MW01530457

ADVANCE PRAISE FOR

Superabundantly Alive

Thomas Merton's Dance with the Feminine

Superabundantly Alive: Thomas Merton's Dance with the Feminine is a refreshing addition to Merton studies. As this book bears witness, each person who reads Merton attentively finds a magic mirror in which he or she sees both a familiar and a transfigured face – a face of surprise, a face unmasked, a face freed from fear.
— **Jim Forest**, author of *Living with Wisdom: a biography of Thomas Merton*

Susan McCaslin and J. S. Porter have given us in this book their heart-felt appreciations of Thomas Merton as gifted *and* imperfect human being, brilliant writer, and intimate friend of his readers. Their synergy as collaborators is infectious: fresh, personal, sassy, substantial. They invite us, their readers, to join with them in 'the general dance of the universe' to which Merton invites us all."
— **Donald Grayston**, past president of the Thomas Merton Society of Canada and of the International Thomas Merton Society

This splendid gallimaufry by two poet-essayists is part riff, part meditation, part invention, part testament, but withal, a brilliant kaleidoscope of impression, insight, and inquiry. The many lineaments of love, desire, and memory, the many strands of 'lived theology,' and the many stages of human and divine maturation are explored with a fetching honesty. A liberating read.

— **Michael Higgins**, Vice-President for Mission and Catholic Identity, Sacred Heart University, CT; his most recent biography is *Jean Vanier: Logician of the Heart* (2016)

... *Superabundantly Alive* gives us a wholly unique reading of Merton's legacy, a "theology of encounter" in flesh and freedom... Approach this book with "beginner's mind" and you cannot help but be drawn into the fire of divine-human vulnerability, rendered vividly, theopoetically, iconically, in a kind of literary-visual mandala — always evocative, sometimes provocative, and everywhere reverberant with hope. McCaslin and Porter have penned one of the finest and most original works on Thomas Merton in many years. It is not just Merton who gazes from these pages, but it is Wisdom-Sophia, the God of grace and mercy, who dares us each moment into loving communion and solidarity with the world.

— **Christopher Pramuk**, author of *Sophia: The Hidden Christ of Thomas Merton*, awarded the International Thomas Merton Society's 2011 Thomas Merton Award

Using different lenses and creating their own 'word dance,' seasoned writers McCaslin and Porter offer us a potpourri of fresh insights about Merton that creates both artistic tribute and epistolary conversation with Tom and with 'M.' — an unconventional approach that maintains its 'centre of prayer-poetry-praise.'

— **Dr. Monica Weis** SSJ, professor emerita of English at Nazareth College, former Vice President of ITMS, and author of *Thomas Merton's Gethsemani* (with Harry L. Hinkle) (UPK, 2005), *The Environmental Vision of Thomas Merton* (UPK, 2011), and *Thomas Merton and the Celts: A New World Opening Up* (Wipf and Stock, 2016)

Superabundantly Alive: Thomas Merton's Dance with the Feminine is a strong, distilled meditation on the life and oeuvre of a remarkable poet-monk whose works of spirit illuminated a turbulent period of 20th century American history.

In a compelling series of essays, the authors navigate the many corners of the 'uncaged mind' of this pragmatic mystic – gender equality, the wisdom of the East, capitalism, war and peace, the relationship between solitude and community, the sacred feminine – with great verve and clarity. They point out Merton's love of and sensitivity to nature, which would qualify him as a precursor in the ecological field.

The book is particularly insightful on Merton's ongoing journey toward the true self, his evolution from flight from the world toward openness and engagement with the social and political problems of his era and what it ultimately means to be fully alive and awake... The authors also explore Merton's brief love affair with 'M.' near the end of his life, calling it a breakthrough in his spiritual journey [which] helped him bridge the duality of male/female into an inner wholeness.

In sum, the authors of this thoughtful, readable study show the reader how Merton, by sharing his brokenness, inspires all of us to embrace our wounded selves as we each climb...toward mystery and greater love. *Superabundantly Alive* offers a rich encounter with the heart-mind-soul of a modern spiritual master.

– **James Clarke**, a poet and retired Ontario Superior Court Justice who has published over twenty collections of poetry, including *Stray Devotions* (Novalis, 2018)

SUPERABUNDANTLY
ALIVE

Thomas Merton's
Dance with the Feminine

Superabundantly Alive

Susan McCaslin & J.S. Porter

FOREWORD BY Lynn Szabo
AFTERWORD BY Jonathan Montaldo

For Frances,

out of the "hidden wholeness"

blessings , Susan.

McCaslin

WOOD LAKE

Editor: Ellen Turnbull
Proofreader: Pattie Bender
Designer: Robert MacDonald

Photograph of Thomas Merton by John Lyons. Used with permission of the
Merton Legacy Trust and the Thomas Merton Center at Bellarmine University.

Library and Archives Canada Cataloguing in Publication
McCaslin, Susan, 1947-, author
Superabundantly alive: Thomas Merton's dance with the feminine /
Susan McCaslin & J.S. Porter; foreword by Lynn Szabo; afterword by Jonathan Montaldo.
Includes bibliographical references.Issued in print and electronic formats.
ISBN 978-1-77343-035-5 (softcover). – ISBN 978-1-77343-146-8 (PDF)
1. Merton, Thomas, 1915-1968. 2. Merton, Thomas, 1915-1968 – Friends and associates.
3. Merton, Thomas, 1915-1968 – Relations with women. 4. Trappists – U.S. – Biography.
I. Porter, J. S., 1950-, author II. Title.
BX4705.M542M345 2018   271'.12502   C2018-903756-3   C2018-903757-1

Text Copyright © 2018 by Susan McCaslin and J.S. Porter
All rights reserved. No part of this publication may be reproduced – except in the
case of brief quotations embodied in critical articles and reviews – stored in an electronic
retrieval system, or transmitted in any form or by any means, electronic, mechanical,
photocopying, recording, or otherwise, without the prior written permission of
the publisher or copyright holder.

Published by Wood Lake Publishing Inc.
485 Beaver Lake Road, Kelowna, BC, Canada, v4v 1s5
www.woodlake.com | 250.766.2778

Wood Lake Publishing acknowledges the financial support of the Government of Canada
through the Canada Book Fund for its publishing activities.
Wood Lake Publishing acknowledges the financial support of the Province of
British Columbia through the Book Publishing Tax Credit.

Wood Lake Publishing would like to acknowledge that we operate in the unceded territory
of the Syilx/Okanagan peoples, and we work to support reconciliation and challenge the
legacies of colonialism. The Syilx/Okanagan territory is a diverse and beautiful landscape of
deserts and lakes, alpine forests and endangered grasslands. We honour the ancestral
stewardship of the Syilx/Okanagan people.

GOLD

Printing 10 9 8 7 6 5 4 3 2 1
Printed in Canada

CONTENTS

For my grandsons, Kaizen, Marshall,
and Blake. I want them to understand why
their grandfather spends so much time reading, thinking about, and writing about
a monk from Kentucky.

JSP

For the two beloveds who have
inspired me most: my husband, Mark,
and our daughter, Claire.

SM

Foreword

LYNN R. SZABO

In these fruitful days of Merton scholarship, we are well-advised to lift our heads from our desks briefly in order to reflect on Merton the human being. How often those of us who have devoted our minds to his thought have also gathered to listen to the stories told by those who knew him best. We are well aware that the select circle of those voices is quickly closing, so we listen very carefully. We hear about his astonishing, sharp, and hilarious sense of humor amidst the carefully drawn portraits of his "uncaged mind." We hear of his ability to "see around corners," his prophetic understanding of social inequities, and his profound concern for the America that he foresaw well ahead of what we observe today.

This book offers an engaging and compelling inquiry into all these many aspects of Merton's "alphabet." In a composite of creative, imaginative writing and penetrating, thoughtful discussion of Thomas Merton and his strikingly fascinating life, two well-recognized poets, Susan McCaslin and J.S. Porter, offer us a lively and captivating reading of their finely-woven responses to this famous poet-monk. It seems rightly appropriate that their book appears on the heels of the centenary (2015) of Merton's birth and the 50th anniversary year of his death, when some new, even novel, approaches to Merton scholarship and dialogue are welcome.

Susan is the author of 15 volumes of poetry and a number of non-fiction prose works. Not only does her writing offer readers an entrance to the rich daily life of a practicing contemplative and highly creative poet, it has also received serious academic attention. Neil Querengesser, a critic of Canadian literature, explains her poetics and their impulses. "[P]aradox and ambiguity are at the heart of McCaslin's poetry, held taut between the two poles of theology and literature." With her brilliant spiritual illumination and its attendant embrace of the feminine Wisdom in both realms, she radiates the sapient qualities that resonate with Merton's own and accredit her as a creative and scholarly benefactress of this work. Her voice has been called "playful and joyous" in addition to all its other temperaments. In this volume, you will find a most pleasurable amalgam of these characteristics and you will be left with a richer, larger sense of the presence and person of Merton and his inestimable value to his readers.

In the marvelous likelihood that poets search for and find each other, J.S. Porter has joined Susan for the pilgrimage of looking at Merton from original and fascinating perspectives. His two well-known and highly-favoured prose volumes, *Spirit Book Word: An Inquiry into Literature and Spirituality* (2001) and *Thomas Merton: Hermit at the Heart of Things* (2008), reveal his "fine critical mind" and "wise odyssey into the very soul of writing," as Keith Garebain has so aptly concluded. Porter is a reader's writer whose ingestion and digestion of words and spirit make him an authentic and authoritative responder to Merton's extensive corpus of poetry and prose. He brings a depth and breadth of creativity that allows him to open mind and heart to the reader as a place to sit with Merton in what I would call serious fun. Here, poetry and prose collapse into spirit and amazement – the lexicon of Merton's "unbroken alphabet."

When I received the already well-drawn drafts of the manuscript for this book, I quickly realized that its combination of fact and fantasy would go far beyond my more limited scholarly imagination. I briefly hesitated at the doorway to this realm, and then almost immediately understood that it was Merton's own. With the genius of his Renaissance capacities, he could inhabit scholarly writing with its generic requisites while remarkably architecting his own creative and contemplative universe, what James Finley has called Merton's "Palace of Nowhere." There, Merton resided as prolific poet and cloistered monk in the dual vocations that permitted and problematized his existence.

Merton remains a significant and public intellectual of ubiquitous influence whose work continues to become known to the North American social and cultural consciousness. More than 50 years ago he was featured in *Life* magazine (1966), much to his superiors' dismay. Yet, in one of the ironies of history, in his address to the American Congress in 2015 Pope Francis claimed Merton as a "great American," along with Abraham Lincoln, Martin Luther King, and Dorothy Day.

In their absorbing dialogue "The Divine and Embodied Feminine," the axis of this volume, McCaslin and Porter discuss the women in Merton's life. These women provided "embodied flight, a mystical awakening, and a new grounding" in writing about his experience of the female in its absences and presences throughout his complicated and heart-breaking search for love – from his mother to his riveting relationship with M., the still-mysteried nurse with whom he fell in love several years before his tragic death. Reflecting what McCaslin experienced when, at age 21, she was astonished into reverence by her reading of Merton's famed *The Seven Storey Mountain: An Autobiography of Faith* (1948), the convergences and intersections of her own mysticism and Blakean scholarship, along with her deep interest in "Hagia Sophia," the female Wisdom of God, align appositely, even providentially, with Merton's own as they evolved throughout this search. Porter joins them to form an exquisite trinity of love in this grace-filled approach to Merton and his "doubts and questions and obsessions, his marginality and his humanness," as Porter describes them. Having been a reader of Merton for more than 40 years, Porter represents a male voice that comes as close to apprehending Merton's deepest wounds and their healing wisdom as any I have found.

From this centre, the book reaches backward into the wonder of the "unbroken alphabet" and its lexicon of "spirit book word" created by Porter's resplendent account of Merton's own reading, and the library of thought and prophecy it creates in the landscape of Porter's mind and poetics. He designs for us a delicate and intricate web of relations between reader and writer. In it is spun the weight of Merton's intellect and spirit and the beautiful tapestry of inflections of Porter's own. With curiosity and alluring flourishes of insight, Porter delights and instructs us in the school of study and formation that was Merton's act of "turning toward the world." For non-religious readers, this is the best of Merton's monastic legacy.

Reaching forward, McCaslin's "Grotto of Sophia Ikons" invites us to encounter the "saints" of Merton's inner cathedral. Designed in the typology of graphics by Afton Schindel, these concrete poems are "ikons" from McCaslin's spiritual imagination awaiting our interpretive attendance in their sacred presence. *Superabundantly Alive* is a remarkably innovative collection, streaming with playful wit and penetrating wisdom from its opening moments where Porter and McCaslin stand alongside each other as poets, to McCaslin's concluding essay, "Sophia Awakening Merton, the Trees, and Me," which recounts her participation in the saving of an old-growth forest in her neighborhood, motivated by her political activism resonant with the spirit and protest of Merton's own critique of progress, war, and capitalism in mid-century America.

This book's epigraphs provide its hermeneutics. I had reservations about its title until I realized it is a direct quotation from Robert Lax's deeply personal and spiritually intimate recognition of Merton's poetry. In "Harpo's Progress: Notes Toward an Understanding of Merton's Ways," Lax describes not only Merton's poetry but the man himself as "superabundantly alive." Indeed, McCaslin and Porter have defined this description in their captivating and enchanting account of the writer/mystic who now comes into his second century of stature and significance "[a]live and burning to the end" in the words of Boris Pasternak.

1.

A Dream of Thomas Merton

SUSAN MCCASLIN

How is it the monk (unhabited) is not surprised,
sitting cross-legged on a patch of earth
trading jokes and cold beer?

Talk of Martin Luther King, Osama, fallen towers,
nothing new under the sun

(except his arch eyes, a high-energy discharge).

"Jesus was the kind of doctor
who would heal anyone who asked—
criminal, insane. No flinching or thinking of bounds."

He pronounces his own new name—
"Threshold dweller"—
hopping like Raven across portals.

Waking, I think how straightaway
I felt his mettle, knowing he had been fed fire—
I, grain.

Thomas Merton in Las Vegas

Thomas Merton flies into the paved desert, the neon sun, the wishing-well of America, on a DC-9. He wears an old jean jacket and a new pair of cowboy boots. He spies the mountains gouged for casinos, the rivers dammed for light bulbs, the churches on every block. *One pull and you can change your life* a figure on a billboard announces. Merton thinks to himself, *the Devil dresses and speaks so well*. In his room he makes notes. Drawers contain Gideon Bibles and bingo chips, the television instructs viewers in blackjack, and the hallways play Muzak. He decides to go for a walk through the palm trees and the traffic. He looks for monks. He finds instead the cocky and the complacent. He notices a bumper sticker. *This isn't reality. This is America.* The heat beats down on his balding head and he limps back to the hotel on the strip. He enters the lobby with a Bob Dylan line in his head. "Money doesn't talk, it screams." As Peter Pans and true believers pull the one-armed bandits, Merton thinks a single thought before an extended prayer and a long sleep. The heart of darkness lurks in spotless lighted streets that repel the night, while 24- hours-a-day enter-tainment centres inject amnesia in sugar-coated promises that never countenance doubt.

—J. S. Porter

Why Merton Matters Now

Will it come like this, the moment of my death?
Will You open a door upon the great forest and set my feet
upon a ladder under the moon, and take me out among the
stars?
— Thomas Merton, *The Sign of Jonas*

A BOOK FLIES OFF A SHELF

In 1968, when I was an undergraduate majoring in English Literature at the University of Washington in Seattle, a hardcover copy of *The Seven Storey Mountain* (1948 edition) by contemplative author Thomas Merton practically spun off the shelf of a used bookstore into my hands. That well-worn, heavily annotated volume of Merton's best-selling spiritual autobiography still nestles in my bookshelf as one of my most treasured possessions.

Around that same time, the photos of Merton suggested a roguish, middle-aged monk roughly of my parent's generation. Now that I am over 70, the monk who died in Thailand in 1968 at age 53 seems young. Yet he remains for me a master of the spiritual path. The journey I began with Merton at the age of 21 has become a lifelong engagement.

The Seven Storey Mountain was compelling to me then because it told in evocative, poetic language the story of a young man's quest for meaning and purpose. It extolled renunciation of the world of outer success and material progress. It embodied a flight, a mystical awakening, and a new grounding. I had temporarily abandoned my childhood religion (but not my faith) to become a hippyish Vietnam War protestor, so the book had great appeal and spoke to my ideals.

From childhood I had been attracted to both the poetic and the mystic paths. Accounts of visions, transformations, and direct experiences of the divine drew me in. I had begun to read the European mystics in university, beginning with John of the Cross and Teresa of Avila. Then William Blake became one of the subjects of my studies in graduate school, and I came to see myself as "a Blakean." To my delight, I learned that Merton had done his master's thesis on William Blake. Merton's gift to me was to validate and contemporize these visionary and mystical streams.

Merton led me not only to mysticism, but to its central practice, meditation, or what he called contemplative prayer. You might say that as a poet and a scholar I've been in a heart-mind-soul clench with Merton ever since. I've dreamed about him, written poems inspired by his works and life, and even had a vision of him in the afterlife as a fully-realized unitive teacher. For me, Merton isn't just an academic pursuit; he is a spiritual mentor.

His books on contemplative prayer have helped awaken recognition in the West and throughout the world of the need for a non-dogmatic, grounded spiritual practice embedded in daily life. His writings continue to encourage people within and without traditional religions to plumb their own inner depths and engage with issues of social justice.

As an English and creative writing instructor at Douglas College in New Westminster, British Columbia, I went on to write poems and scholarly papers on Merton, some of which explore his love of William Blake, his attraction to the poet Rainer Maria Rilke, and his brief friendship with poet Denise Levertov. Whenever I think I'm ready to move on and turn to other subjects, he sneaks up on me again. My delving into his mystic-poetic affinities led to a depth study of Merton's long prose poem "Hagia Sophia," a meditation on the feminine figure of Holy Wisdom from early Jewish, Christian, and Eastern Orthodox sources.[1] Merton also opened me to the wisdom of the East and its Zen sages and wisdom teachers, both ancient and modern.

A HERMIT-MONK LAYS HIS FINGER ON
THE PULSE OF THE WORLD

It is important that Merton wasn't a systematic theologian or philosopher, or a person of fixed ideologies and dogmas, but a spiritual pragmatist, an imperfect pilgrim on the path to integral being. Increasingly, contemplation and action became his yin and yang, inseparable and complementary. He upheld the tension of the contraries, the vital dynamic between interior development and social action. Though cloistered for most of his life, through his widely circulated Cold War Letters where he spoke out against the Vietnam War, and his essays and poems where he took positions on racism and nuclear weapons, he became increasingly a person of his times. The mystic and the political activist were for him non-dual aspects of a single consciousness. Thus, Merton inspired me to engage in a successful initiative combining the arts and activism to help save an endangered rainforest near my home.

Merton lived with apparent contradictions. He wrote in *The Sign of Jonas* that he found himself "travelling toward [his] destiny in the belly of a paradox."[2] He is a loquacious, apophatic (one keenly aware of the limits of language), and logocentric poet (one who regards the word as a fundamental expression of reality) whose words spring from and return to silence. Yet balancing the writer with the monk or solitary who speaks from the margins is characteristic of his mystic predecessors who likewise aspired to the heights and depths of mystical unity. John of the Cross and Teresa of Avila, for example, were simultaneously mystics and socially engaged, prolific writers. The mystics Merton studied throughout his life modelled for him how to live at the pivot between silence and speech and become a font of peace and cauldron of roiling energy.

A YOUNG WOMAN NAMED PROVERB CLASPS
MERTON IN THE MARKETPLACE

In a journal entry of February 1958, Merton relates a dream-vision in which Holy Wisdom in the form of a young, dark-haired Jewish woman passionately accosts him in the street.

> I am embraced with determined and virginal passion by a young Jewish girl. She clings to me and will not let go... I ask her name and she says her name is Proverb.[3]

This mystical experience has to be understood in the context of Merton's later Fourth and Walnut revelation in 1958, described in *Conjectures of a Guilty Bystander*, where he records an epiphany about the shining light emanating from ordinary humans (mostly women, in the context of his journals) on a street corner in Louisville. It is also informed by his sophianic studies around the same time. Proverb (Sophia, Wisdom) is not merely God in a skirt or God's feminine counterpart or assistant. She is an essential presence and power ("consubstantiality") within the divine Unity. Wisdom isn't simply playing at the foot of the throne as God's consort but is the *Ousia* or dark ground of both being and becoming. Beyond even the dualism of being and non-being, she is part of the interplay of eternal consciousness within the self and the natural world. The recovery of the sacred feminine is an essential strand in Merton's spiritual legacy. For me, his embrace of the sacred feminine (in himself, the world, and in each person) is one of his central contributions.

The full story of Merton and Proverb includes the psycho-spiritual drama of his own healing, and the restoration of the feminine in himself. Despite his struggles with various aspects of feminine presences in his life (the loss of his mother at the age of six, his admittedly profligate relations with women at Cambridge University and before his conversion to Catholicism, and his taking refuge in a patriarchal community), the divine feminine kept breaking through in his dreams and writings. Divine feminine Wisdom was implicitly present in his early veneration of Mary, as evidenced by his "Song for Our Lady of Cobre" (1944), and she presents herself ever more insistently and intimately as he matures. It may have been that losing his mother at such a young age led him unconsciously to set forth on a lifelong quest to reclaim and embody the feminine.

Poetry seems to be Merton's primary means of healing and transformation. He may be more acknowledged as a writer of prose, but his prose is often as highly charged, layered, and resonant as his poetry. Poetic prose and actual poems are embedded throughout his journals. Though Merton's poems are not as widely read as his contemplative writings, I feel they will last as long as his prose and be rediscovered in ever-new contexts.

For me, "Hagia Sophia" (1962), a prose poem centered on the feminine divine, is Merton's masterwork. It enacts his steady recovery of the peace-making feminine through his Proverb-Sophia dreams and sophianic explorations. It presents the poet-speaker at his most vulnerable, rising from sleep in a hospital bed at the call of Wisdom's voice to make his way on the earth. It's no accident that for Merton the recovery of wisdom and the reconnection to the earth go hand in hand, as Wisdom is the power of embodiment, of incarnation or "being in the world." Furthermore, "Hagia Sophia" links the recovery of the feminine to the world's salvation. Here Merton's peace work and the divine feminine are tightly interlaced. As he puts it in a journal entry of January 1961, "Faith in Sophia, *natura naturans*, [is] the great stabilizer today – for peace."[4] And one of the books that nourished this prose poem is Russian theologian Paul Evdokimov's *Woman and the Salvation of the World* (1945).

Merton's embrace of the feminine wasn't wholly a matter of his readings and dreams. There is additionally the matter of the young nurse Merton refers to in his journals as M., with whom he fell in love in 1966. In the portions of his journals from June of that year, which Merton titled "A Midsummer Diary for M,," he reflects on this transformative period in his life.[5] Despite not being able to commit himself to quotidian life in marriage with Margie (for complex reasons we might never untangle), I see his relationship with her not as a lapse, but as an emotional and spiritual breakthrough. He writes, "I will never really understand on earth what relation this love has to my solitude. I cannot help placing it at the very heart of my aloneness, and not just on the periphery somewhere."[6] This was the first time Merton was able to imagine living with a woman as co-equal, loving and being fully loved.

> I felt that if we had only had a chance, we could have grown magnificently together into a beautiful organism of love; we could have slowly healed and strengthened each other, brought out all that was waiting to develop, that was blocked, that was held back by society.[7]

Shortly after what Merton called the "amputation" of his relationship with M. and the resumption of the solitary life, he entered into a lively 18-month correspondence with budding feminist theologian Rosemary Radford Ruether. The letters that emerged from this brief friendship add another real-life dimension to his dialogue with the feminine.[8] Ruether was a feisty young woman who disagreed with Merton on the value of monasticism and took him to task for being what she saw as a recluse. She felt he should have been more directly engaged with the world. Yet Ruether's cheeky feminism may have been just the palliative Merton needed. Though some of her analyses seem dismissive of Merton's deep need for solitude, I read with delight her ability to approach the revered man as an equal. "I'm just as fleshy as you, baby, and I am also just as much of a 'thinking animal' as you."[9] I am equally impressed with Merton's humility and willingness to open himself to her critiques.

The point is that Merton moved beyond merely studying and writing about the sophianic traditions to engage authentically with a strong-minded woman who was anything but the soft and sweet feminine stereotype. His correspondence with Ruether, which followed upon his emotional and sensual relationship with M. and preceded his journey to the East, reveals that Merton opened himself to many aspects of the feminine. It would have been easy for him to pull rank on Ruether and take a "you don't really know who I am" stance, but he makes himself vulnerable. Though Ruether's challenges to Merton don't take into account the full extent of his activism through his writings and letters, she penetrates to the heart of his existential dilemma. At one point he surprisingly asks her to be his "confessor" and admits that there are times when he'd like to abandon monasticism.

Integral to Merton's embrace of the feminine is his lifelong embrace of nature and nature's embrace of him. He had an early and lifelong sensitivity to what we now call the ecological field. He read Rachel Carson's *Silent Spring* not long after her seminal environmental work on pesticides first appeared. His love of nature and Thoreau-like observations permeate his journals. When reading Merton, we are never far from the natural world as the matrix that births and sustains us and on which we are entirely dependent. For him, this matrix is another manifestation of Sophia.

A Man from the West Stands Barefoot before the Buddhas

Merton's stillness and absorption before the giant statues of the Buddhas at Polonnaruwa, as recorded in *The Asian Journal* just before his death, sum up the cumulative power of his witness: integration, a movement into unitive consciousness where the dualities of subject/object, self/other disappear and we are "all already one, but imagine that we are not."[10] His life and works point to integration not only of the self (male and female, matter and spirit) but also of the mystical traditions of East and West. Merton's universality at the end of his life is not a facile syncretism but a hard-won unity that builds on every step of his sojourn through monasticism and the Christian and global mystical traditions. At the gate from which heaven and earth spring, he becomes a citizen of the world. The most startling and significant aspect of Merton's life is his ever-increasing inclusivity – his steady evolution out of parochial religion into a universal interspirituality, or what the Vietnamese Buddhist monk Thich Nhat Hanh calls interbeing.

Evolving Mystic

How do we reconcile the contradictions posed by the many faces of Thomas Merton? It is time to look not just at the masks and personas of Merton's outer personality as memoirist, poet, theologian, contemplative, activist, calligrapher, photographer, naturalist, activist, journal-keeper, jazz aficionado, etc., but also at the broad sweep and long trajectory of the *geist* of his longing.

Pope Francis, in his speech to the UN in New York on September 24, 2015, acknowledged Merton's continuing relevance. He spoke eloquently of Merton's contribution to interreligious and interspiritual dialogue in a time when dialogue is the thing most needed. Along with Abraham Lincoln and Martin Luther King, Jr., Francis named both Merton and Merton's friend and correspondent Dorothy Day, founder of the Catholic Worker Movement, as spiritual leaders who have worked indefatigably for justice and peace.

A nation can be considered great when it defends liberty as Lincoln did, when it fosters a culture that enables people to

"dream" of full rights for all their brothers and sisters, as
Martin Luther King, Jr. sought to do; when it strives for
justice and the cause of the oppressed, as Dorothy Day did
by her tireless work, the fruit of a faith which becomes
dialogue and sows peace in the contemplative style of
Thomas Merton."

It is remarkable that throughout his relatively short lifespan,
Merton kept expanding, maturing, going beyond himself. One
hundred years after his birth, he shines not merely as a progressive, contemplative monk and prolific religious writer, but as a
universal spiritual teacher. The whole of his journey is a dramatic action-parable of a movement toward integration with
the nameless mystery some call God, others, Unitive Being or
the One. However named, it is that place of ultimate mystery
from which language flows and where words and concepts bow
to the plenitude of silence that transcends and includes them.

Like each of us, Merton was imperfect, but he kept moving beyond dualities and false either/ors. One does not have to
choose a favourite work, the poetry over the prose, or the later
over the early works. What matters is the constant evolution
of both his life and his work – the always-surging, expanding
process. The way he makes a gift of his own fragility gives us
hope that each of us, with our own finitudes, flaws, and fail-
ures, may also touch holy ground. He is not removed from us,
but a close friend. The core of our being, like his, intersects
with the luminous core that he called the *point vierge*, or "point
of nothingness" that is "pure diamond."¹² When we read him,
we are invited to linger at this juncture, this *no place* where we
don't know exactly who we are, where we're going, or what
our final destination might be. We know only that we are always here, always now, always interconnected. He expresses it
best at the end his life in *The Asian Journal* where he states,
"We are already one.¹³

1   Susan McCaslin, "Merton and Hagia Sophia (Holy Wisdom)," in *Merton & Hesychasm: the Prayer of the Heart*, ed. Bernadette Dieker & Jonathan Montaldo (Louisville, Kentucky: Fons Vitae, 2003), 235-260.

2   Thomas Merton, *The Sign of Jonas* (San Diego: Harcourt & Brace, 1981), 11.

3   Thomas Merton, *A Search for Solitude: The Journals of Thomas Merton*, Vol. 3: 1952-1960, ed. Lawrence Cunningham (NY: HarperSanFrancisco, 1996), 176.

4   Thomas Merton, *Turning Toward the World: The Pivotal Years*, ed. Victor A. Kramer (NY: HarperSanFrancisco, 1996) 91. Christopher Pramuk cites and discusses this statement extensively in his *At Play in Creation: Merton's Awakening to the Feminine Divine* (Collegeville, Minnesota: Liturgical Press), 35.

5   Thomas Merton, *Learning to Love: The Journals of Thomas Merton*, Vol. 6: 1966-1967, ed. Christine M. Bochen (NY: HarperSanFrancisco, 1997), 301-348.

6   Merton, *Learning to Love*, 327.

7   Ibid., 326-327.

8   Mary Tardiff, OP, ed., *At Home in the World: the Letters of Thomas Merton & Rosemary Radford Ruether* (Maryknoll, New York: Orbis Books, 1995).

9   Tardiff, *At Home in the World*, 49.

10   Thomas Merton, *The Asian Journal of Thomas Merton*, ed. Naomi Burton, Brother Patrick Hart, & James Laughlin (NY: New Directions, 1968; 1975), 308.

11   Pope Francis, quoted by Grant Gallicho, in *Commonweal* (Sept. 24, 2015). https://www.commonwealmagazine.org/blog/pope-francis-congress-be-your-best. Accessed March 3, 2016.

12   Thomas Merton, *Conjectures of a Guilty Bystander* (NY: Doubleday, 1968), 158. Merton writes, "Again, that expression, *le point vierge*...At the centre of our being is a point of nothingness which is untouched by sin and by illusion, a point of pure truth, a point or spark which belongs entirely to God, which is never at our disposal... It is like a pure diamond, blazing with the invisible light of heaven. It is in everybody, and if we could see it we would see these billions of points of light coming together in the face and blaze of a sun that would make all the darkness and cruelty of life vanish completely... I have no program for this seeing. It is only given. But the gate of heaven is everywhere."

13   Thomas Merton, journal entry, June 22, 1966, *Learning to Love*, 328.

2.

The Unbroken Alphabet of Thomas Merton

J.S. PORTER

On November 1, 1968 in Dharamsala, India, just weeks away from his death in Bangkok, Thomas Merton records a Tibetan saying.

> The milk of the lioness is so precious and so powerful that if you put it in an ordinary cup, the cup breaks.[1]

This saying has haunted me for more years than I care to admit. I have carried it in the backpack of my mind the way one carries essentials for a trip but is not sure when an item might be put to use. I think I now know the use. Merton is the lioness. His milk (message) is so precious and powerful that if you put it into a book, or any other container, it breaks free.

Pick up a magazine on yoga, or Buddhism, or running, or cycling, and he'll be there. Pick up a book on religion, or spirituality, or politics, or philosophy, and he'll likely be there too. Thomas Merton has a surprising capacity to pop up in places you may not expect. He is still alive in our culture; a quiet presence in recited prayers at addiction meetings, for instance. I've heard his words on love at weddings and even at funerals. His words encourage, challenge, scold, provoke, console, and humble.

What you are about to read in this chapter is a personal response to another's life and an attempt to answer a question. Who was Thomas Merton? Or, who is he? *Is* seems more appropriate. Merton is a living presence for many, including me. So much so that I once tried to speak in his voice in an attempt to capture something of his rich complexity.

> seeds within words
> some grow, some wilt
> all are conceived
> if not in you, in someone else
> if not here, elsewhere
> all at some point flower
>
> I am polyglot
> not sure which language is native
> which country is home
> and all my skins are itchy.[2]

When I wrote the above words, I wasn't sure if I was talking about Merton or about myself.

Forty years on from my first reading Merton, I'm still making notes on his great energy and vitality and celebrating his all-too-human nature. I'm still captive to his emblems, raids, and conjectures. I still read him for his insights on race (the white race in particular), technology, Eastern philosophies, the Bible, war and peace, and his appreciation of Latin American cultures. I'm still awed by his power and inspired by his legacy.

His early life – with the experiences of losing his mother, his father, and then his brother – shows an intimacy with loss. Yet his middle years through to his final days point to a refusal to let loss define who he is. He is made of what the rest of us are made of. He knows desire, longing, fear, regret, and – a small word with enormous power – *mercy*, used the way some of us use the word *grace*: what catches us when we fall, what forgives us when we can't forgive ourselves. Merton is as ordinary and broken as we all are, but he is able to communicate more of his spirit and personality than just about any writer I can think of. His thinking, as evidenced particularly in his journals, is daring, compassionate, self-critical, inclusive, and integrated.

Pope Francis, in his address to the US Congress on September 22, 2015, says it best, even if he does use the past tense. "Merton was above all a man of prayer, a thinker who challenged the certitudes of his time and opened new horizons for souls and for the Church. He was also a man of dialogue, a promoter of peace between peoples and religions."[3] That's why he matters to me, and that's why I want to tell my grandsons about him.

I like to retell a story about Amiya Chakravarty, poet and consulting editor for Merton's *Asian Journal*. Chakravarty recalls meeting Merton in front of their hotel in Calcutta. Merton raises his head and greets his friend, "I'm looking at everything." And he was. He was looking at "cars, rickshaws, beggars...the daily office crowd...the clouds and kites in the sky." Everything. Then Chakravarty's remembrance goes straight to his friend's legacy. "... [H]e challenged colour barriers, religious tyranny, economic justice, took up the cause of suffering minorities and majorities. That morning I saw his patience and his oneness with life in a teeming city."[4] That's also who Merton is and why he continues to matter to those who engage with him on the page.

In his August 21, 1967 letter to Dom Francis Decroix in response to a request from Pope Paul VI for a "message of contemplatives to the world," Merton shares his life's mission.

I have become an explorer for you, a searcher in realms which you are not able to visit... I have been summoned to

explore a desert area of man's heart in which explanations
no longer suffice, and in which one learns that only experience counts."[5]

Merton is at his core an explorer, a searcher, and a seeker. He is
someone who struggles to find meaning in the confusion that
exists around him and sometimes within himself.

Merton seems driven to experience life as fully as possible
and then to record his experiences, wherein he tastes life once
again. His collected writings fashion one of the longest and full-
est accounts of what it is to be a human being – awake, aware,
alive (artistically, politically and spiritually) – in the 20th century. If you gathered all his journals together, public and private, they would constitute the approximate equivalent of
Proust's 3,500-page serial novel, *In Search of Lost Time*, or Anaïs
Nin's collected *Diaries*.

The thirst for experience took Merton into politics, poetry,
inter-faith dialogue, and love. "Broadening of horizons in every
direction" is one of his self-constructed phrases. That's what he
did throughout the 1960s. He broadened himself in all directions: "political leftism, peace (Gandhi), study of the Orient,
creative work, writing, publishing..."[6] He hurled himself at the
world. He drew it and photographed it. He wrote about it, argued with it, bore witness to it, and loved it.

In the last year of his life, Merton started up a journal called
Monks Pond. He whimsically explained his editing process in a
letter to the American poet Louis Zukofsky: "No money involved anywhere." Instead, "Poems, creative things, Asian texts,
blues, koans, ghost dances, all to be crammed into four issues."[7]
The journal, like a comet, blazes for a short time – four seasons, beginning in spring and ending in winter. It broadens in
all directions.

Key Letters in the Merton Alphabet

All of us live our days within broken alphabets. These alphabets may be scrambled, or they may have missing letters, or letters that remain unanimated or unfulfilled. Not all letters become words. Not all words become flesh. The missing or incomplete letters in everyone's alphabet remind us of the chasm between what we reach for and what we're able to grasp.

Broad in his interests, deep in his probes, Merton wished, it seemed, to play every letter on the keyboard's alphabet. But there are some letters that time and circumstance didn't't permit Merton to fully develop – C for Child, for instance. Merton, one can imagine, would have loved to have held hands with his own children or carried them in his arms. Not to do so was a loss in his life. I can say from having carried my grandsons and held their hands that there are few experiences in life so precious and irreplaceable as the touch of a child.

Within our alphabets, we gain and lose. Disappointments and blessings abound. The surprise in Merton's alphabet is not so much his normalcy in being unable to fully animate certain letters, but his successful intermeshing of so many of his passions and interests. The surprise is not that his alphabet is broken, but the extent to which it is unbroken.

Merton's friend Robert Lax sees the interconnectedness of everything Merton does, and in an October 12, 1963 letter he exhorts him to produce more art, both visual and linguistic.

> write more poems and make more calligraphies:
> the poems help the calligraphies, the calligraphies
> help the poems; the poems and the calligraphies
> help the manifestos; you will see, you will see.[8]

Whether in politics (his manifestos), or visual art (calligraphies and photography), or in his poetry and essays, everything has a "hidden wholeness." All Merton's work seems to come from, and arrive at, the same place. Robert Lax calls this place *prayer*.

Merton is not only a poet-monk. A multi-hyphenated man, he is also a thinker-monk, a photographer-monk, a calligrapher-monk, a translator-monk, a teacher-monk, and so on. In a late journal, he emphatically declares why he's here. "I know I have to read, and understand, and think, and grasp, and experience."[9] He reads broadly and deeply, understands many things, and thinks and grasps and experiences a great deal. And he frames his experiences in compellingly simple language that makes strangers – readers – think that they are his friends and fellow-travellers on his journey.

His signature is not only *I write, therefore I am*, but also *I love, therefore I write*.

Z FOR ZORBAMONK

Of those who personally met Thomas Merton, whether in flesh, spirit, or print (and putting aside his best friend Robert Lax for the moment), several stand out for their insights into his character.

Brother Patrick Hart, Merton's private secretary during Merton's final years, says, "Never in my life have I met anyone with such a variety of interests, so many. And he could see connections among them all. That was the thing – he was always bringing out the connections."[10]

This connecting mind is much in evidence in his writing. Take this simple example from his journals, for instance: "After dinner – read the Prometheus Bound of Aeschylus... It is like Zen – like Dostoevsky – like existentialism – like Francis – like the New Testament. It is inconceivably rich."[11] Like and like, connection and connection and connection. You also see the connective mind beautifully at work in "Rain and the Rhinoceros" where rain, the sixth-century Syrian monk Philoxenos, and Eugene Ionesco's play "Rhinoceros" are brought into a verbal field of interactive play and contemplation.

Biographer Michael Mott illustrates Merton's unifying mind with a summarizing sentence from Merton's final poetic work, *The Geography of Lograire*: "Cargo Cults, Bantu myths, a play on Cook's landing in the South Pacific, missionaries, Ghost Dances, outrageous advertisements in The New Yorker, Mayan fertility dances, as well as much else..."[12] That's our omnivorous monk.

Scholar, writer, one-time visitor, and fellow-Kentuckian Guy Davenport observes, "When he wrote about the Shakers, he was a Shaker. He read with perfect empathy: he was Rilke for hours, Camus, Faulkner... I wonder whether there has ever been as protean an imagination as Thomas Merton's."[13]

Art critic Roger Lipsey, in *Angelic Mistakes*, adds: "... [Merton's] visual art ... arose from the surplus in him – a surplus of energy and intelligence, inquiry and camaraderie."[14]

An inquisitive mind, an empathetic imagination, a surplus of energy: Thomas Merton was a Zorba monk, a man of tremendous energy and exuberance. Picture Anthony Quinn dancing on the beach in the film "Zorba the Greek." "If man is to live, he must be all alive, body, soul, mind, heart, spirit,"[15] Merton writes, in words worthy of Zorba.

Merton in his work and personhood was "superabundantly alive." For Lax, his major characteristic was

(gen

u

ine)

live

li

ness.[16]

Lax describes Merton's way of movement as a series of small explosions.

he did walk with joy. he walked explosively: bang bang
bang, as though fireworks, small & they too, joyful, went off
every time his heel hit the ground...he walked with joy,
bounced with joy: knew where he was going.[17]

Poet and friend Ron Seitz describes his laugh: "Tom, the great
laugher. God, was he ever that! Open-mouthed 'Oh Ah Ha' with
head thrown back, hands on hips." He taught Seitz, and a good
many others, including myself, "the chomp chomp umm good
lip-puckered 'Aaahhhh!' to life."[18]

He moved, said Lax in "Harpo's Progress,"

with speed &
direction
certainty
& joy[19]

So: he walked like Zorba, laughed like Zorba, and at times danced
like Zorba. Sometimes he even sounded like Zorba. When an
enterprising man writes to ask him to make a contribution to a
book on success, Merton indignantly replies that he has spent
his life "strenuously avoiding success." (He says his best-seller
The Seven Storey Mountain came from "naïveté and inattention"
and was "a pure accident.") He teasingly goes on to say that if
he had a message for his contemporaries it would be: "Be anything you like, be madmen, drunks, and bastards of every shape
and form, but at all costs avoid one thing: success."[20]

Merton, however, was more than an embodiment of
Kazantzakis' fictional dynamo in the novel *Zorba the Greek*. He
was also the "boss" character (the narrator of the novel): the
eternal student, the intense scholar, the driven intellectual, the
disciplined writer. (Boss was reading Dante when Zorba first
met him, something Merton did as a young man.) You need

both characters in one body – the student and the dancer – to approach Merton's integrated wholeness of being.

One of the key moments in the novel for me occurs when the playful Zorba asks the serious-minded Boss if he knows how to dance.

> 'Do you dance?" he asked me intensely. "Do you dance?"
> "No."
> "No?"
> He was flabbergasted, and let his arms dangle at his sides.
> "Oh, well," he said after a moment. "Then I'll dance, boss. Sit further away, so that I don't barge into you."
> He made a leap, rushed out of the hut, cast off his shoes, his coat, his vest, rolled his trousers up to his knees, and started dancing."[21]

Merton danced when Joan Baez offered to drive him to Cincinnati to see M. when M. got off the night shift, and he danced in his best writings. He knew how to dance and he knew how to laugh. The Merton that emerges from comments by friends seems a good deal more Zorba-like – more daring in thought and more spontaneous in person – than the rather tame, domesticated character one meets in some scholarly or pious commentaries on his life.

Merton had an energy that allowed him to produce vast quantities of work. What he once said about the bard can be applied to himself. "Shakespeare is always doing marvelous things that are the products not of any recognizable personality, but of sheer imaginative overflow, a brilliant excess."[22] Merton was a man in overflow, of brilliant excess. An immense sea. When you tire of one bay, you can swim to another.

The vastness of him:
Thousands of drawings
Thousands of letters to over two thousand correspondents
Over a thousand pages of poetry in the *Collected Poems*
Hundreds of essays
Hundreds of photographs
50+ books in his lifetime, and more now with new assemblages

Merton was a harsh critic of the world – "Half the civilized world makes a living by telling lies"[23] – and a great lover of the world – "The whole purpose of the monastic life is to teach men to live by love."[24] He held within himself the tensions his friend and fellow-correspondent Czeslaw Milosz articulated in a poem.

I was stretched between contemplation
of a motionless point
and the command to participate
actively in history.[25]

Merton somehow found the balance to live the *vita contemplativa* and the *vita activa*, although as his fellow peace-activist and biographer James Forest rightly says in his Introduction to *Living with Wisdom: A Life of Thomas Merton*, "He spent far more time at Mass, in prayer, and in meditation than in writing books and letters or doing anything else likely to bring him to public attention."[26] And for all the temptations to unpack himself from Gethsemani, untether himself from monastic life, and go elsewhere, he learns the wisdom of the poet's words.

Task: to be where I am.
Even when I'm in this solemn and absurd
role: I am still the place
where creation works on itself.[27]

Merton had an amazing gift for friendship. His friendship with Robert Lax in particular is one of the great literary and spiritual friendships of the 20th century. But as Merton withdrew from the world, he seemed to burrow into it more deeply. As he let go of many things, he clasped the hands of friends more firmly.

He seemed to be always under construction, always in process. He tattooed on his flesh, so to speak, a single radical idea: you grow and change or you pay the price for staying the same. Merton chose to grow. In his journals, he writes of "[t]he need for constant self-revision, growth, leaving behind, renunciation of yesterday, yet in continuity with all yesterdays... My ideas are always changing, always moving around one centre, always seeing the centre from somewhere else. I will always be accused of inconsistencies – and will no longer be there to hear the accusation."[28] Any reader of a specific Merton work or utterance needs to ask in rapid succession, "What's the date? What's the mood? Who's the audience?"

He was natural (a word he frequently and affectionately applied to his father in *The Seven Storey Mountain*), spontaneous, generous, open, vigorous, and funny. Lax said in conversation with James Harford, "He never wrote me a letter that wasn't funny."[29]

Robert Lax reads the life and character of Thomas Merton personally, impressionistically, intimately. He reads him playfully, generously, holistically. He emphasizes Merton's physicality as much as his spirituality, his humour as much as his theology. As Lax biographer Michael N. McGregor rightly intuits about Merton, "nowhere is he more *alive* on the page than in his writing to Lax."[30] If you listen closely to their playful voices you can still hear them chortle.

To be fully understood and appreciated by a reader is a rare thing; to be understood and appreciated by a friend who reads discerningly I suspect is even rarer. At Merton's centre, as at

Lax's centre, was prayer-poetry-praise – all three together as a single stroke of the brush or a single breath on the page. The supreme compliment that Lax paid to Merton was that he (Lax) was most himself when around him. In *Journal C*, written shortly after Merton's death and several years after the deaths of Ad Reinhardt and other friends, Lax records this entry: "i remember the people i loved (who have died) or who've just disappeared   remember their traits as though it were a sacred duty."[31]

In his prose poem "Remembering Merton & New York," Lax clearly remembers Merton as though it were a sacred duty. He catalogues their haunts in the city, the bars they drank in, the streets they walked on, the writers he liked, the movies they went to, the music they listened to.

He celebrates salient aspects of Merton's personality:

Bright?
Quick?
Sensitive?
Yep.
Funny?
Yep.[32]

Lax's memory of meeting Merton at Columbia University had to do with the warmth and friendliness of Merton's body posture. "...Jacobson took me over and introduced me. Merton looked up and shook hands, and it was really an amazing meeting right away. It was the friendliest look, the friendliest handshake I'd ever remembered."[33] When Zorba shakes your hand, you remember it.

V FOR VOICE

We no longer have Merton with us with his rapid-fire speech, his pinball walk, his Zorba handshake. What we have is his voice on the pages of his books. His voice is warm and inclusive. The first sentence he writes to Boris Pasternak on August 22, 1958 might stand for most of his encounters with friends and strangers. "Although we are separated by great distances and even greater barriers, it gives me pleasure to speak to you as to one whom I feel to be a kindred mind."[34] Merton generally seeks common ground and attains it by his welcoming voice.

The American philosopher Ralph Waldo Emerson insisted on reading books to experience those moments in which we hear a voice that we recognize as proceeding from the same centre as our own voice. I read for voice, for a voice that enriches my own inner voice. When I first read Merton, he seemed to speak from my centre, and, over time, he amplified the music of my inner voice.

Voice has always been my pathway to intimacy. I read people and books by voice. How someone sounds tells me how someone is. Within seconds of speaking to my mother or sister on the phone, I think I can give a fairly accurate reading of their mood and general well-being. I learned to do this from a young age. Reading my father by voice alone was always more difficult. He was the most gifted actor in the family and could, if he chose, disguise the feelings in his voice.

When I taught literature at college, I wanted to get to know my students. I wanted to hear their personal stories and have a sense of their dreams. When I write, it's intimacy with readers I seek. I thirst after connection. I hunger for close relationship. I see the same hunger and thirst in Merton.

Most of my writing is a personal response to my reading. I seek in my reading and writing what the novelist Doris Lessing calls "a small personal voice."[35] Thomas Merton gives me "a small personal voice." For me, that's where intimacy resides. Following the sound of a voice, one enters a mind, a heart, a soul.

I have a sense that the core of Merton is "The Intimate Merton." (Brother Patrick Hart and Jonathan Montaldo chose this phrase as the title for their one-volume cull of the seven posthumous journals that highlights significant moments in Merton's short life.) If you find a few pages in the Merton canon where he doesn't speak intimately, you can probably skip over them.

When I want to hear that distinctive Merton voice, I turn to "Day of a Stranger," in which Merton gives an account of his days in his hermitage to a Latin American audience. My copy of the book version of the essay (edited and introduced by Robert E. Daggy) consists of a small sheaf of pages accompanied by Merton's photographs – icons, a desk, a wagon wheel, a wicker chair, chopped wood, a bench, a wheelbarrow, a rain bucket, and other simple human-made objects. In this short volume, Merton reveals that his days at the hermitage during the last few years of his life are full of birdsong and poetsong. His language is direct and strong. "The hills are blue and hot. There is a brown, dusty field in the bottom of the valley. I hear a machine, a bird, a clock. The clouds are high and enormous."[36] Simple, declarative, evocative sentences.

Merton walks his readers through some of his rituals.

> Washing out the coffee pot in the rain bucket…Spray bedroom (cockroaches and mosquitoes). Close all the windows on south side (heat). Leave windows open on north and east sides (cool). Leave windows open on west side until maybe June when it gets very hot on all sides. Pull down shades. Get water bottle. Rosary. Watch. Library book to be returned."[37]

Later, he adds more details.

> I sweep. I spread a blanket out in the sun. I cut grass behind the cabin. I write in the heat of the afternoon. Soon I will bring the blanket in again and make the bed…Soon I will cut

bread, eat supper, say psalms, sit in the back room as the
sun sets, as the birds sing outside the window..."

In his concluding sentence, he moves from the natural world
and his rituals within it to the threatening mechanical world
outside (bombers on their way to Vietnam).

Meanwhile the metal cherub of the apocalypse passes over
me in the clouds, treasuring its egg and its message.[38]

He depicts his outer world and his inner world equally as facets
of the real.

I am out of bed at two fifteen in the morning, when the
night is darkest and most silent...I find myself in the primordial lostness of night, solitude, forest, peace, a mind awake
in the dark, looking for a light..."

Then he falls into poetry.

A light appears, and in the light an ikon. There is now in the
large darkness a small room of radiance with psalms in it.
The psalms grow up silently by themselves without effort
like plants in this light which is favorable to them. The
plants hold themselves up on stems which have a single
consistency, that of mercy, or rather great mercy...In the
formlessness of night and silence a word then pronounces
itself: Mercy."[39]

Merton's mind moves from the physical to the spiritual; or rather,
his mind dwells on the mingling of the spiritual with the physical. He knows that there are other words and other realities
aside from mercy – Blood. Guile. Anger. – vying for dominance

in the society around him. He alludes to the racial strife in Selma and to "the atomic city, from which each day a freight car of fissionable material is brought to be laid carefully beside the gold in the underground vault which is at the heart of the nation." He knows destructive words – "hate, the opening of the grave, void" – have power, but he also knows that "mercy, great mercy" is the last word. That is Merton's faith. "The birds begin to wake. It will soon be dawn."[40]

He rests and breathes easy in the conviction that he has "an obligation to preserve the stillness, the silence, the poverty, the virginal point of pure nothingness which is at the centre of all other loves."[41]

Of the writers whom I've internalized in some way, none has more intimately engaged me than Thomas Merton. When reading him, I convince myself that he is writing a personal letter to me. What Hemingway said of Gertrude Stein – that she had "found a way of writing that was like writing letters all the time"[42] – fits my understanding of Merton. Much of his best writing is letter-like – personal, intimate – and seems addressed to a single reader: you, me. There is a naturalness to his voice, a lack of strain, an easy breathing. What he once said about the poet Zukofsky pertains to himself. "He never reaches to make anything 'musical' or 'poetic,' he just touches the words right and they give the right ringing and tone."[43]

Merton's voice drew me in almost 40 years ago when I first began to read him and it's what keeps me coming back to his work. In 1988, in *The Thomas Merton Poems*, I attempted to borrow the spirit of his voice on the 20th anniversary of his death. Twenty years after that I revisited his life and work in *Thomas Merton: Hermit at the Heart of Things*. I've tried to say farewell on numerous occasions, and somehow his voice calls me back.

Merton has a way of speaking whereby the intimacy of his voice convinces you that you're a co-writer of his words rather than a mere listener to them. In his best writings, in his most personal confessions, he establishes an extraordinary degree of intimacy between writer and reader. He re-enacts Whitman's "Camerado."

> I give you my hand!
> I give you my love more precious than money,
> I give you myself before preaching or law;
> Will you give me yourself?
> will you come travel with me?..."[44]

In the letter to Pasternak which I've already quoted, Merton speaks of his identification with Pasternak's writings. "I feel as if it were my own experience, as if I were you... It is as if we met on a deeper level of life on which individuals are not separate beings."

Merton speaks brother to brother, brother to sister. He doesn't speak as an authority; he speaks as a beginner. He doesn't lecture from the pulpit; he speaks from the table at which the two of you are seated. "He shows you his cuts and bruises in words as simple as bread, as full-bodied as wine."[45] And when he finishes talking, you ask yourself, *Is he talking about himself or about me?* He tears down the barrier between the self and the other. His voice is your voice. As he says in the preface to the Japanese edition of *The Seven Storey Mountain*, "I seek to speak to you, in some way, as your own self."[46] Or, as he writes in "Six Night Letters," one of his 18 love poems to M.,

> Writing to you
> Is like writing to my heart
> You are myself [47]

Throughout his body of work, he frequently dissolves the borderline between self and other.

You don't read Thomas Merton; you hear him. He speaks directly to your ear. You don't read him; you meet him. I can't think of another writer who expresses more of who he is and what he stands for than Merton. He's able to put his body on the page, his soul on the page. He invites you into his life by using a kind of tonal alchemy. *I am you*, he says time and again. *And you are me. What moves in you moves in me.*

Merton's mission as an explorer of the desert regions of the heart is to undergo change and transformation and then to write about the changes and transformations in such a way that you wonder if you're part of the transformation too. His is the diction of comradeship, the discourse of brotherliness. Merton, in his own phrasing, is "the incarnation of everybody,"[48] incarnated not as strength but as fragility, not as certainty but as doubt, not as centrality but as marginality.

In reading Merton, I'm reading a living, struggling human being who is undergoing the same crises and problems that I'm facing. His best words are written in the fires of personal experience. One feels called to be a witness to his life. Whoever touches his books, in Whitman's phrasing, touches a man. The book as flesh. As Emerson says about the French essayist Montaigne, "Cut these words, and they would bleed; they are vascular and alive."[49] The word as flesh.

If I had to pick just one sentence from the Merton canon that instantly defines his character, it would be this one: "This is simply the voice of a self-questioning human person who, like all his brothers, struggles to cope with turbulent, mysterious, demanding, exciting, frustrating, confused existence in which almost nothing is really predictable, in which most definitions, explanations, and justifications become incredible even before they are uttered, in which people suffer together and are sometimes utterly beautiful…"[50] That's the voice. That's why I keep coming back to hear more of it.

J FOR JOURNALS

Thomas Merton writes lively sentences.

How about the spectacular sentence that begins *The Seven Storey Mountain*, Proustian in its sinuousness? "On the last day of January 1915, under the sign of the Water Bearer, in a year of a great war, and down in the shadow of some French mountains on the borders of Spain, I came into the world."[51] Or this simple, powerful sentence from *New Seeds of Contemplation*: "Every moment and every event of every man's life on earth plants something in his soul."[52]

Merton seems to plant seeds most abundantly in his notes, the short pithy utterances often found in his journals or journal-like essays such as "Day of a Stranger." He had the self-knowledge to know where his strengths lay. On September 16, 1958 he notes, "Galley proofs of *Secular Journal* make it clear to all that my best writing has always been in Journals and such things – notebooks."[53] Many readers make their first acquaintance of Merton through his journals, and among his most respected works are the journal *The Sign of Jonas* and the journal-like *Conjectures of a Guilty Bystander*.

Journals are a form of autobiography for Merton, a way of keeping track of his days and preserving ideas and experiences that are important to him. Autobiography, in journal form or otherwise, "begins with a sense of being alone" and "is an orphan form"[54] according to the English art critic, essayist, and novelist John Berger. And by his early 20s Merton was the complete orphan: mother, father, grandparents, brother, all gone. The self, in such a predicament, sends notes to itself that it is still alive and still developing, even without familial roots. These messages reassure and encourage; hence the pep talks you frequently hear in Merton's journals.

The notes also self-explore, self-interrogate, and self-criticize. It's not easy being a monk with the mental equipment of an artist; it's not easy being a man without a woman, or a man without a child. But because Merton has the talent to find clarity within his colliding tensions, his unachievable yearnings, his swerves and shifts in emotion and attachment, and to then share it with the rest of us, we all gain from being witness to his struggles.

Merton awaits an enterprising John Robert Colombo to come along and do for him what he did for Northrop Frye: compile the best sentences from a vast body of work. I can readily envisage a *Thomas Merton Quote Book* as a companion volume to *The Northrop Frye Quote Book*. Such a book would draw heavily from Merton's journals, both those published in his lifetime and the posthumous private journals. You can extract gems from all the journals, but the private ones for me have the most resonance. Here is Merton at his unrehearsed, unselfconscious, uncensored, raw best, picking through the bricolage of his mind.

On Proust

Proust and memory: to Proust experience seems to be valuable only after it has been transformed by memory. That is, he is not interested in the present...The 'present time of things present' was unbearable. What kept attracting him was the 'present time of things past.'[55]

On Marx's insight into women

It is certainly true that man is most human, and proves his humanity, by the quality of his relationship with woman.[56] (This, in Marx, surprised me.)

On 'deerness'

I watched their beautiful running, grazing...The thing that struck me most: one sees, looking at them in movement, just what the cave painters saw — something that I have never seen in a photograph. It is an awe-inspiring thing — the Muntu or 'spirit' shown in the running of the deer, the 'deerness' that sums up everything....[57]

On solitude

The only solitude is the solitude of the frail, mortal, limited, distressed, rebellious human person, made of his loves and fears, facing his own true present...[58]

"In his journals," says Canadian scholar Ross Labrie, "Merton came closest in a verbal medium to the spontaneous self-expression that he achieved in his calligraphies."[59] Of all the journals, the one I most frequently return to is *The Asian Journal*, his last take on the world. I agree with Robert Lax's assessment that here Merton is "...most himself, most keen & observant, witty, lost, (found), erudite, enlightened, clean, natural, free, mature...."[60]

Compiled by his editor Naomi Burton Stone, his private secretary Brother Patrick Hart, and his publisher James Laughlin five years after Merton's death, *The Asian Journal* draws on three separate notebooks: "A," the public journal intended for publication; "B," the private journal; and "C", the pocket notebook. *The Asian Journal* fulfills Merton's declared ambition, recorded on July 17, 1956, to write an inclusive and expansive book. "And I have always wanted to write about everything...a book in which everything can go. A book with a little of everything that creates itself out of everything. That has its own life. A faithful book. I no longer look at it as a 'book.'"[61]

As in the tradition of the poet Basho, with whom Merton shares a haiku mind (a mind at play in its jumps and multiple connections), whatever Merton sees or thinks or feels or dreams he records. "Two white butterflies alight on separate flowers. They rise, play together briefly, accidentally, in the air, then depart in different directions."[62] Birds and butterflies receive as much comment in *The Asian Journal* as the Buddha statues in Polonnaruwa, or American politics.

In the democracy of the journal form, the lowly share space with the mighty in the quick of Merton's mind. "Gandhiji's

broken glasses... Johnson has stopped the bombing. Two mag-
pies are fighting in a tree."[63] In the journal, like life itself, one
thing mixes with another. Alongside his notes on encounters
with the Dalai Lama and his readings of scholars on Buddhism,
beggar girls touch the heart. "The little girl who suddenly appeared at the window of my taxi, the utterly lovely smile with
which she stretched out her hand, and then the extinguishing
of the light when she drew it back empty."[64]

A grab bag, a potpourri, an Irish stew, *The Asian Journal* is
not only a Book of Everything, it's also a Book of Last Things –
last notes, last photographs, last poems, last personal encounters, last readings, speeches, letters, and prayers. Love pours
across the pages: love of people, love of nature, love of life. His
final journal reads more like a new beginning, a new integration
of thought and feeling, than it does as an unexpected ending to
a full life.

W FOR WRITER

Perhaps Merton's career as a writer begins with his mother's
book about him as a child – *Tom's Book* – a book of firsts, including first words. Might her short "biography" be the seed of his
autobiographical penchant throughout his life?

Born in France, he spends his early years there. According
to his mother's notes, he greets the world bilingually.

> Oh sun! Oh joli!
> bonjour buddha
> Monsieur Wind [65]
> *[my arrangement in poetic form]*

His lifelong fluency in the language and his French poems and
translations speak to his respect for his French beginnings.
Some pages in *The Seven Storey Mountain* shine with love for
his birthplace.

Thomas Merton is a writer-monk and an artist-monk. Secular France gives greater weight to one side of the hyphen than the other. A plaque on his family home in Prades reads, *Ici est né Thomas Merton Écrivain Américain* (This is where the American writer Thomas Merton was born). The French town of St. Antonin, near where Merton attended school, has a plaque on a walkway that reads, *Thomas Merton, Écrivain* (Thomas Merton, Writer), as if "writer" is sufficient for nationality. Religious America tends to shift the emphasis to the monk side. You need both sides of the hyphen to encompass Merton.

Merton was made from paper and pen, from typewriter and ink. Appropriately, most of the front covers of his posthumous journals show his body, and sometimes his face, covered in his own handwritten script. When your family tree is cut down, as Merton's was, you re-seed yourself from the only soil you have – your own. And you use your principal gift – that of using reading and writing to understand yourself and the world.

These are the writings I return to:

"Love and Need: Is Love a Package or a Message" (essay)
from the posthumous *Love and Living*
"War and the Crisis of Language" (essay) in *Passion for Peace: The Social Essays*
"Hagia Sophia"
"Louis Zukofsky – the Paradise Ear" (essay) from *The Literary Essays*
"Notes on Solitude" (a meditation from *Disputed Questions*)
Opening the Bible
Day of a Stranger (a Peregrine Smith Book, with Robert Daggy's important introduction and some of Merton's photography)
"Midsummer Diary for M. "
Eighteen Poems (also for M.)
Emblems of a Season of Fury

"Signatures: Notes on the Author's Drawings" from *Raids on the Unspeakable*

His translations of Cortés and Chuang Tzu

The pages from *The Seven Storey Mountain* concerning his father and Merton's time in France

His final talk, "Marxism and Monastic Perspectives," from *The Asian Journal*

His essay "Cargo Cults of the South Pacific" from *Love and Living*

"Rain and the Rhinoceros" from *Raids on the Unspeakable*

"The General Dance," the last chapter of *New Seeds of Contemplation*

Cold War Letters and selections from *The Courage for Truth: Letters to Writers*, along with letters to and about young people

A Swiftian satire – his *Original Child Bomb*

What did Merton mean by "writing"? In his *Journals*, he makes his definition clear to himself and to the reader. "For to write is to love: it is to inquire and to praise, or to confess, or to appeal."[66] He links writing to love. As early as December 20, 1939, Merton is able to say to himself, and hence to us as eavesdroppers on his private confessions, "I only know I am writing well about the things I love: ideas, places, certain people: all very definite, individual, identifiable objects of love..."[67]

He also links writing to his practice of being a monk. In *The Sign of Jonas*, Merton comes to the realization that "writing is one thing that gives me access to some real silence and solitude... Also I find that it helps me to pray, because when I pause at my work I find that the mirror inside me is surprisingly clean and deep and serene and God shines there and is immediately found, without hunting, as if He had come close to me while I was writing..."[68]

Later in the same book Merton writes, as if coming to new

insight while in the act of writing, "I must also put down on paper what I have become... To be as good a monk as I can, and to remain myself, and to write about it: to put myself down on paper, in such a situation, with the most complete simplicity and integrity, masking nothing...without exaggeration, repetition, useless emphasis."[69] Few writers more completely communicate their fullness – blemishes and beauty marks alike – than Thomas Merton.

Sometimes Merton doubted that he was a monk; he never doubted that he was a writer. But what kind of writer? Certainly he was autobiographical. You could argue that almost all of Merton's books, whether in poetry or prose, are chapters in an ongoing autobiography terminated only at death by an electrical accident in Bangkok. In his journal notes of 1939 he records that, "The big monuments of these years are all autobiographies," among which he includes "Joyce, D.H. and T.E. Lawrence, Thomas Wolfe, Saroyan, G. Stein, etc." Then, using the royal we, something he rarely does, Merton says, "I guess where we really know how to talk is in autobiography. We can't write *Iliads* or Greek plays but we can write autobiography – and poetry."[70]

He tried his hand at novels in his early years, but none worked out successfully. He didn't seem particularly adept at conceiving a character other than himself in ever-shifting mood, tone, and temperament. He would have concurred with Emerson. "... [N]ovels will give way, by and by, to diaries or autobiographies – captivating books, if only a man knew how to choose among what he calls his experiences that which is really his experience and how to record truth truly."[71] Merton knew what his real experiences were, and how to write about them truly.

The journal is the form Merton frequently turns to in his autobiographical explorations and record-keeping, but poetry is no less central to his development. He is first and last a poet.

He reads, writes, translates, and comments on poetry. He thinks poetically – thought not as analysis, argument, or calculation, but thought as play, experiment, or meditation.

His first published work (late 1930s) consisted of poems. His first published book was *Thirty Poems* in 1944. This was four years ahead of the publication of *The Seven Storey Mountain*, the first installment of his continuous autobiography. Merton's first major piece of prose writing (his master's thesis in 1939) concerned the English poet William Blake and is included as an appendix in *The Literary Essays of Thomas Merton*. During the last weeks of his life he was busy writing "Kandy Express," a fascinating mixture of travel notes and haikus in *The Asian Journal*, as well as revising the long poem *The Geography of Lograire*. Poetry, poetry, and poetry – his first and last greetings to the world.

And what is poetry? My poet-friend Susan McCaslin has as good a definition as I've come across: "Poetry is an entering into mystery, the zone of the unspeakable that desires to be spoken."[72] Poetry doesn't pin down, it explores. It doesn't give answers, it questions.

Merton was a talented reader of poetry, translator of poetry (mostly from the Spanish of Latin American poets, but sometimes from the French and the Portuguese as well), and writer of poetry. Many of his best poems are found in a slim volume called *Emblems of a Season of Fury* (1963). In *Emblems,* you have the beautiful meditative prose poem "Hagia Sophia" along with the memorable "An Elegy for Ernest Hemingway."

In his journals, Merton acknowledges the need to infuse everything he does with poetry, "regarding poetry as more essentially my work (instead of an accidental pastime) in working. Poetry – includes Journal and poetic prose – records of poetic (creative) instants."[73] The son of artists – his father a landscape artist in the style of Cézanne and his mother gifted in interior design – making words and images was as much a part of his life as prayer and meditation. He once said, half-jestingly and very revealingly, "It is not much fun to live the spiritual life with the spiritual equipment of an artist."[74]

In a letter dated April 27, 1967, Merton advances a strong opinion on the future of poetry to the Venezuelan poet and scholar Ludovico Silva. Merton regards the future very positively. "The poets have much to say and do: they have the same mission as the prophets in the technical world. They have to be the consciousness of the revolutionary man because they have the keys of the subconscious and of the great secrets of real life."[75]

Merton possesses a poetic and religious mind – a unifying and synthesizing mind – and to have a religious mind is to respond to the world poetically in praise and gladness. Poetry deals with concretes, with the things of the world, and is quite different from the irreligious mind, which "is simply the *unreal* mind, the zombie, abstracted mind, that does not see the things that grow in the earth and feel glad about them, but only knows prices and figures and statistics. In a world of numbers, you can be irreligious, unless the numbers themselves are incarnate in astronomy and music. But for that, they must have something to do with seasons and with harvests..."[76]

Authentic religion must incarnate itself in the ordinary day-to-day activities of human beings. As Merton eloquently writes to Rosita and Ludovico Silva on April 10, 1965, presaging his "Day of a Stranger,"

> That is where the silence of the woods comes in...and one
> works there, cutting wood, clearing ground, cutting grass,
> cooking soup, drinking fruit juice, sweating, washing,
> making fire, smelling smoke, sweeping, etc. This is religion.
> The further one gets away from this, the more one sinks in
> the mud of words and gestures.[77]

One's words must be as alive as the domestic actions one undertakes, and as the silence that surrounds them.

In his first private journal, Merton distinguishes between the logic of language and the logic of mathematics. "The former is something like experience: it follows it closely, is not rigid but supple, and imitates life. The logic of mathematics is abstract, more certain, if you like, but achieves certitude at the expense of truth. That is, it is less real."[78] Tellingly, in his published journal, *The Secular Journal*, he puts the emphasis on "the logic of the poet" in language reminiscent of William Blake, rather than on the logic of language.

> The logic of the poet — that is, the logic of language or the experience itself — develops the way a living organism grows: it spreads out toward what it loves, and is heliotropic, like a plant. A tree grows out into a free form, an organic form. It is never ideal, only free; never typical, always individual.[79]

By the time Merton comes to write one of his most significant literary essays, "Louis Zukofsky – The Paradise Ear," he's ready to make the bold assertion that

> [a]ll really valid poetry (poetry that is fully alive and asserts its reality by its power to generate imaginative life) is a kind of recovery of paradise... [T]he living line and the generative association, the new sound, the music, the structure, are somehow grounded in a renewal of vision and hearing so that he who reads and understands recognizes that here is a new start, a new creation.[80]

For Merton, poetry at its finest consists of language "fully alive" with the power "to generate imaginative life" so that readers enter into "a renewal of vision" that offers them "a new start, a new creation." Poetry can re-introduce Eden.

Merton carries his idea of new creation not only into the reading and writing of poetry, but also into the translating of it. In a letter to the Uruguayan poet Esther de Caceres on January 9, 1965, he talks of translating the correspondent's lecture on another Uruguayan poet, Susana Soca. "I have never yet had a moment to translate some of her poems, and I would not want to do this in a rush. Precisely, it would have to be a new creation emerging from communion in the same silence."[81]

In her essay "Encounter in a Secret Country: Thomas Merton and Jorge Carrera Andrade," Malgorzata Poks writes, "It seems that the success of the monk's translating efforts lies in the fact that he did not merely read literature, but *meditated* on it until the deep truths contained in it became part of him, *connatural* with him – a term that Merton the follower of Jacques Maritain applied to the experience of knowledge by identification, in art as much as in religion."[82]

All of Merton's activities around poetry had to do with ingestion, with taking the work into himself so that it became a part of his being. To paraphrase Robert Lax, the reading helps the translating, and the translating helps the writing, and they all together deepen his understanding of the world. He was moving toward a synthesis of poetry and prayer, where the breath of one would infuse the breath of the other.

Poetry as a new start, a new creation, a new imaginative life, need not be as grand and dramatic as T.S. Eliot's *Four Quartets* or Rilke's *Duino Elegies*. New life and vision can come from a poem as simple and earthy as Merton's "The Reader."

Lord, when the clock strikes
Telling the time with cold tin
And I sit hooded in this lectern

Waiting for the monks to come,

And the monks come down the cloister
With robes as voluble as water.
I do not see them but I hear their waves.

It is winter, and my hands prepare
To turn the pages of the saints...[83]

In these simple, honest lines and images, Merton gives the reader a taste of the quiet rituals and camaraderie of monastic life. The poem is "a new creation" in its sound-pictures of praise. "Robes as voluble as water" is a particularly striking poetic image. The poem was selected by the editors for inclusion in *Twentieth-Century American Poetry* along with "For My Brother: Reported Missing in Action, 1943." In the anthology Merton keeps company with Wallace Stevens, William Carlos Williams, Denise Levertov, and Muriel Rukeyser, among many others.

T FOR TURNS

"Turn, Turn, Turn." It's a song written by Pete Seeger in the 1950s and made a hit by The Byrds in 1965. Seeger took the ancient Ecclesiastes text and put it into contemporary wording.

There is a season... And a time for every purpose, under Heaven.[84]

It's Thomas Merton's life song as a man of many turnings. Merton is a modern day Odysseus, although many of his journeys were more internal than external. He takes dramatic turns in his spirituality, reading, reach for love, and politics.

Merton's most life-changing turns are first to the Catholic Church and then to monastic life. The wayward Protestant becomes the pious Catholic. Received into the Catholic Church at Corpus Christi in New York City in 1938, he enters the Abbey of Our Lady of Gethsemani on December 10, 1941, a calling he's loyal to for 27 years until his death. Gethsemani gives him the time and space in which to do his work. He becomes a priest in 1949. He's made Master of Scholastics in 1951 and Master of Novices in 1955. Both of these positions are teaching functions that require a great deal of talk from a man sworn to silence.

He turns toward serious reading in his Columbia University years, notably when he stumbles upon Etienne Gilson's *The Spirit of Medieval Philosophy* in Scribner's, a New York City bookstore, in February 1937. Before you can become a "medieval monk" you need to read about being one. He continues with his intellectual and spiritual development and reads Aldous Huxley's *Ends and Means* (Huxley makes mysticism interesting and Eastern thought equally fascinating) and Jacques Maritain's *Art and Scholasticism* (Merton later befriends Maritain and his wife Raïssa). These are Merton's life-changing reading experiences, comparable to Proust's discovery of John Ruskin or St. Augustine's radical redirection after reading Paul's Epistle to the Romans.

To be young and reading in New York City in the 1930s at a time when both reader and city were in full bloom must have been heavenly. Merton's reading experiences evoke another reader in another city – the young Hemingway in Paris in the 1920s reading the Russians for the first time. Gilson, Huxley, and Maritain make their imprint on the young Merton in New York as Turgenev made his imprint on the young Hemingway in Paris.

According to Virginia Woolf in her essay "Hours in a Library," the true reader is someone young. "The great season for reading is the season between the ages of eight and 24."[85] Her words bear an element of truth in the case of Merton's reading life, for at Columbia a young Merton encounters the Christian poet and mystic William Blake, about whom he writes his master's thesis. And at the urging of the Hindu monk Brahmachari, he begins reading Christian classics, including Augustine's *Confessions* and Thomas à Kempis's *The Imitation of Christ*.

Woolf, however, may not be entirely right in Merton's case. He has a second revolution in his reading when he turns to Zen and the East in the early 1960s. He reads and then meets Zen authority D.T. Suzuki; he reads and then meets John Wu, who assists him in his translation of *The Way of Chuang Tzu*. As a result of his reading, Merton ends up writing three additional books on Eastern thought: *Zen and the Birds of Appetite*, *Mystics and Zen Masters*, and the final notes that evolve into *The Asian Journal*.

Merton turns to politics in a letter to Dorothy Day on August 23, 1961. "...I don't feel that I can in conscience...go on writing just about things like meditation... I think I have to face the big issues, the life-and-death issues..."[86] Throughout the 60s, he is much more than a "guilty bystander" (one of his self-characterizations). He is a political activist who writes on the key social issues of his time: race, technology, and war. I'll say more about this in a minute, but love trumps politics and must be spoken of first.

In the summer of 1966, Merton turns toward love – the love of a particular individual who bears the initial M.

Love "is a certain special way of being alive." It's "an intensification of life, a completeness, a fullness, a wholeness of life."[87] Merton learns this insight from his relationship with M., a student nurse who cared for him in a Louisville hospital for a short but transformative time.

He writes in his journal, "I am going to write maybe a new book now, in a new way, in a new language too. What have I to do with all that has died, all that belonged to a false life? What I remember most is me and M. hugging each other close for hours in long kisses and saying, 'Thank God this at least is real!'"[88]

He does write in a new way. We see this clearly in the essay "Love and Need: Is Love a Package or a Message?" that was published posthumously in a grab-bag of essays, *Love and Living*, in 1979. He writes the article in September of 1966. He met M. in April of 1966. Her presence is clearly apparent in powerful Pauline sentences like these, which are inconceivable without her:

> We do not become fully human until we give ourselves to each other in love.
> We do not find the meaning of life by ourselves alone – we find it with another...
> My true meaning and worth are shown to me not in my estimate of myself, but in the eyes of the one who loves me...
> He who loves is more alive and more real than he was when he did not love.[89]

And yet, for all of Merton's immersion in love's life-enhancing power, he ultimately turns in another direction, an old direction. He reaffirms his commitment "...to read, and understand, and think, and grasp, and experience," and to share his discoveries with others. And that, for him, is best done as a monk who writes in a monastery.

Did he lose his nerve? Was he afraid of tarnishing his reputation? (Merton was, after all, by the mid-1960s a monastic "rock star," known throughout the world and relied on as a spiritual mentor by many.) I don't know. But I do know this: he chose to express his love through his writing rather than through a long-term intimate relationship with a particular human being. And yet, things are seldom simple or clear cut in Merton's life. I have it on the authority of the monks at Gethsemani that Merton kept writing to M. after the break-up; he was even writing to her on his Asian journey. Had he lived, would he have resumed the conversation, if not the physical contact? There are reasons for thinking so. Once Merton developed a deep connection in friendship, he seldom let go.

If Picasso had his pink and blue periods, his Trappist look-alike had his Zen period, his love period, and his political period. It's the political period I turn to now in some detail.

The significant year of redirection is 1961. As Merton scholar William Shannon notes, during the summer of 1961 Merton writes three important political tracts: his "Auschwitz poem" published as "Chant to Be Used in Processions Around a Site with Furnaces," in which he enters the mind of a Nazi officer for subversive purposes; his "Original Child Bomb" written in the persona of a journalist understatedly recording the facts leading to the bombings of Hiroshima and Nagasaki and the beginning of the nuclear age; and his essay-letter to Pablo Antonio Cuadra on the dual madness of the United States and the Soviet Union in risking nuclear annihilation.[90] These tracts show an incisive mind grounded in the world and able to see it from the margins with great clarity.

One of Merton's major insights during this time of political turmoil is the identification of the representative personality of the age: the engineer/problem solver/efficiency expert who speaks in a combination of technical jargon and bureaucratic cliché. Merton comes to an understanding of the age's representative human being through his studies of Adolf Eichmann, about whom he writes explicitly on three occasions: first in his "Devout Meditation in Memory of Adolf Eichmann" (1964) in *Raids on the Unspeakable*, then in *Conjectures of A Guilty Bystander* (286-290) in 1965, and finally in his "Epitaph for a Public Servant" (1967) originally written for *Ramparts* and posthumously included in the *Collected Poems*. Merton's three satirical tracts are the partial fulfillment of his declaration to Dorothy Day that he would address "the life-and-death" issues of his time. He also wrote implicitly about the Eichmann personality (or, more accurately, performed the Eichmann-like mind) in "Chants to be Used in Processions Around a Site with Furnaces" (1963).

Merton writes to Day on September 22, 1961 and attaches

his essay, "The Root of War is Fear." The essay appears in the October issue of *The Catholic Worker*. Merton also begins his Cold War Letters, which were 111 letters written between the Berlin crisis and the Cuban Missile Crisis – a time of very real threat of nuclear annihilation. These letters were censored by the monastery between October 1961 and October 1962 because of their political bluntness.

"The Root of War is Fear" continues to have resonance in contemporary culture, showing up, for instance, in Jim Willis's bestseller *God's Politics*, which offers "a new vision for faith and politics in America." Willis quotes Merton in chapter seven: "Be Not Afraid: A Moral Response to Terrorism." You also see Merton's coupling of fear and war in fellow Catholic Michael Moore's *Fahrenheit 9/11*, where a short, animated movie-within-the-movie highlights the history of fear in the United Sates, particularly fear of the Indigenous American and the African-American. You can now add the Muslim to the list of bogeymen.

Perhaps even more relevant to our times is Merton's prose poem *Original Child Bomb: Points for Meditation to be Scratched on the Walls of a Cave*, which offers an historical demonstration of fear leading to mass murder. (One of the rationales for the nuclear bomb at the time was, *If we don't use it, someone else will get it and use it on us*.) First published in Robert Lax's poetry broadside *Pax*, Merton's "*Bomb*" is the work that most forcibly speaks to us now. There were approximately 130,000 people murdered in one day in Hiroshima in 1945. The poem makes that horrific event vivid and memorable by understatement and irony. The reader shudders in response.

You might not expect a monk to be such an astute political commentator. When you live in an environment (a monastery) where there are few distractions – no radios, televisions, or newspapers – you have opportunities for concentration. But how did Merton keep pace with current events? Answer: with a little help from his friends. Merton was well connected to activist friends, from Dorothy Day, "Ping" Ferry, and Edward Rice, to Daniel Berrigan and Jim Forest. Books and articles supplied by Merton's publisher James Laughlin and others allowed him to be well-read in contemporary issues.

In James W. Douglass's *JFK and the Unspeakable,* one of the seminal works on the Kennedy assassination, Merton acts as Virgil in the Underworld, accompanying Douglass through the labyrinths of deceit and deception. Merton not only provides the title of the book, he also provides the political context. The thesis of Douglass's book is that Kennedy was assassinated by the military-information complex of the United States or, if you prefer, the National Security State. As Merton put it in the *Cold War Letters,* and Douglass quotes in chapter one, "...[T]his country has become frankly a warfare state built on affluence, a power structure in which the interests of big business, the obsessions of the military, and the phobias of political extremists both dominate and dictate our national policy." Douglass continues quoting Merton in words that seem to speak to present day America: "It also seems that the people of the country are by and large reduced to passivity, confusion, resentment, frustration, thoughtlessness and ignorance, so that they blindly follow any line that is unravelled for them by the mass media"[91] – or obfuscated by right-wing talk show hosts on radio.

Merton goes on to say, and is again quoted by Douglass, that "[o]ur weapons dictate what we are to do. They force us into awful corners. They give us our living, they sustain our economy, they bolster up our politicians, they sell our mass media; in short we live by them. But if they continue to rule us we will also most surely die by them."[92] Merton saw the darkness clearly.

In his analysis of current affairs in his journal entry on September 9, 1961, he sees the United States as a major obstacle to peace: "...The mixture of immaturity, size, apparent innocence and depravity, with occasional spasms of guilt, power, self-hate, pugnacity, lapsing into wildness and then apathy... You need a doctor, Uncle!"[93]

The difference between our time and Merton's is not the madness – madness seems forever with us – but the lack of voices aligned against the madness. In Merton's day, Christians, from Dr. King to Dorothy Day to the Berrigan brothers, could be counted on to oppose the money interests of the 1% and the political system that supports them. In our time, Pope Francis, among Christians with a public voice, seems almost alone in speaking for the poor and the environment. Many of his fellow Christians, particularly in the United States, are more interested in the "prosperity gospel" (I'm all right, Jack. You look after yourself, do as I do, and you can be successful, too) than the revolutionary gospel of Jesus Christ. They are more interested in personal salvation than collective salvation.

A FOR THE AMERICAS

"With the World in My Blood Stream" is the title of one of Merton's poems to M.

Merton had Europe in his blood, the Americas in his heart, and Asia in his dreams. When his friend Edward Rice (his first biographer) painted Merton, he painted his face with a brown tinge, and blank so that the viewer could impose his own face.[94] As a struggling human being, ever articulate about his struggles, Merton is everybody. Rice's blank-face portrait has light brown shading perhaps to signify that there are more non-whites in the world than whites. Merton knew that, not only intellectually but viscerally; he knew it in his heart.

In his biography *The Man in the Sycamore Tree: The Good Times and Hard Life of Thomas Merton*, Edward Rice presents Merton's understanding of Western and North American "mythdreams," in which we delude ourselves into thinking that others operate out of mythologies while we "are utterly scientific" and "have no myths" (which in itself is one of our principal myths). Rice quotes Merton as saying that the reason communication is difficult across cultures is that we lack "an ability to communicate also with something deeper *in ourselves*... We are out of contact with our own depths. It is our primitive self which has become alien, hostile, and strange."[95]

Merton is a man of the Americas who is interested in "[d]eeper roots, Indian roots. The Spanish, Portuguese, Negro roots also." The shallow English roots are insufficient. The Americas are older than the Anglo experiment on First Nations soil, and richer than efficient administration and technology. "My vocation," says Merton, "is American – to see and to understand and to have in myself the life and the roots and the belief and the destiny and the Orientation of the whole hemisphere."[96] America, for Merton as for Jack Kerouac, wasn't so much a country as it was two continents, a whole hemisphere.

Merton's affection for Latin America doesn't manifest in travel to those countries. He doesn't get to see the landscapes he seems to identify with even though his Nicaraguan friend Ernesto Cardenal invites him to visit; but he writes discerningly of its poets.

Stefan Baciu pays tribute to Merton in "The Literary Catalyst." His essay, published in *Continuum* shortly after Merton's death, summarizes Merton's contribution to Latin American poets. "During the last two decades, Merton was one of the constant and most accurate spokesmen for this realm [the realm of Latin American poetry] through a series of translations without equal in the literature of the United States, or, for that matter, in world literature." Merton "knew how to love, understand, and interpret the Spanish and Spanish-American worlds."

Baciu specifically acknowledges Merton's translations of Alfonso Cortés, César Vallejo, Pablo Antonio Cuadra, and Nicanor Parra, and concludes his remarks with these words:

No one like him had been able to contribute to the literature of United States a 'living anthology' of the most modern literary movements in Latin America. For this he had the
calling, the heart and the knowledge that today almost no
one has in this country. With his death the new literature
south of the Rio Grande lost not only a friend, but also one
of the best and most faithful interpreters.[97]

Further, Robert Daggy, in his introductory essay to *Day of a
Stranger,* reminds us that Merton wrote his day-journal "Day of
a Stranger," his Preface to *Obras Completas,* "A Letter to Pablo
Antonio Cuadra Concerning Giants," "Message to Poets," "Answers on Art and Freedom," "Christian Humanism," "Answers
for Hernan Lavin Cerda," and other works for individual Latin
American friends.[98] "Message to Poets" and "Answers on Art
and Freedom" were written, for instance, for Miguel Grinberg
from Argentina, whom I had the pleasure of meeting, walking
with, and hearing speak at the St. Bonaventure University conference in 1995.

In his Preface to *Obras Completas* (a limited and selected
Complete Works) Merton rises to poetry in his prose. The US

lacks the roots of the old America, the America of Mexico
and the Andes, where silent and contemplative Asians
came, millenniums ago, to construct their hieratic cities. It
lacks the intense fervor and fecundity of Brazil, which is also
African, which smiles with the grin of the Congo and laughs
with the childlike innocence of Portugal. The northern half
of this New World lacks the force, the refinement, the
prodigality of Argentina with all the lyricism of its tor-
mented and generous heart.[99]

Of all his many connections to Latin American writers, Merton
seems to have a special relationship with the poets of Nicara-

gua, that small country which has produced a formidable body of poetry from the time of the influential Hispanic poet Rubén Dario.

Ernesto Cardenal

Former novice under Merton, close friend, and founder of the community of Lake Solentiname, a community for the theology of liberation, spiritual renewal, creative arts, and Nicaragua's poor. Also priest, poet, liberation theologian, Marxist, and Minister of Culture in the Sandinista government from 1979 to 1987. Cardenal writes a fine tribute to Merton entitled "Coplas on the Death of Merton." In volume IV of the *Letters – The Courage for Truth: Letters to Writers* – over half are letters from Merton to Latin American writers, and a whole section consists of letters to Cardenal.

How Merton would have enjoyed the conversations at Lake Solentiname that gave birth to some of the most powerful responses to the Gospels ever recorded.

> The Bible is a constant denunciation of injustice and a constant defense of poor people, widows, orphans... That's the difference between the Bible and all the pagan religions, which considered the world as finished, unable to change, and they were on the side of the status quo, oppression.[100]

Cardenal's words seem to echo Merton's own. "We must never overlook the fact that the message of the Bible is above all a message preached to the poor, the burdened, the oppressed, the underprivileged."[101]

Pablo Antonio Cuadra

Another Nicaraguan for whom Merton writes letters, essays, and translations from the Spanish. One of Cuadra's great poems, "Meditation before an Ancient Poem," in Merton's wording has a flower ask if its scent will survive, and then has the moon ask if it can keep some light after perishing. The poem poignantly ends with these two lines:

> But man said: 'How is it that I end
> And that my song remains among you?'"[102]

Alfonso Cortés

A Nicaraguan poet whom Merton translates and writes a poem about. In a letter to José Coronel Urtecho on April 17, 1964, Merton says of Cortés, "He is a wonderful and symbolic man, perhaps one of the most significant people of our age..." In the same letter he acknowledges feeling "very much a part of the Nicaraguan movement in poetry..."[103] In Merton's *Collected Poems* there are 11 translations of Cortés's poems. Merton's *Emblems of a Season of Fury* contains nine translations plus a poem entitled "To Alfonso Cortés." Merton's reading of Latin American poetry is broad and extensive.

Significantly, Merton's translations of major Latin American voices are still in use 40 years after his death, and several of his Cortés translations are to my knowledge the only published ones in English. Few poems in Merton's translations from the Spanish have the stark beauty and subtle power of "Great Prayer."

> Time is hunger, space is cold
> Pray, pray, for prayer alone can quiet
> The anxieties of void.
>
> Dream is a solitary rock
> Where the soul's hawk nests:
> Dream, dream, during
> Ordinary life.[104]

In a comprehensive anthology entitled *Twentieth-Century Latin American Poetry*, edited by Stephen Tapscott, Merton's translations of Vallejo's "Anger," Cuadra's "The Birth of the Sun," Parra's "Mummies," and Cardenal's "Like Empty Beer Cans" are the poems' voices in English.

E FOR ENCOUNTERS

On July 9, 1965, Merton makes this entry in his journal: "The theology of 'encounter' is not just a phrase. What else is The Acts of the Apostles? The whole of the Christian is The Acts of the Apostles."[105] The theology of encounter isn't a phrase he drops into a journal; it's his way of approaching people. He builds relationships and makes friends. He remembers that spirit comes to us by way of the body. He knows viscerally the truth of Mary Oliver's lines.

> The spirit
> likes to dress up like this:
> ten fingers,
> ten toes,
> shoulders, and all the rest...[106]

Merton's way into ideas is often through flesh, through physical contact. His knowledge of Latin America, for example, deepens through his contact with Latin American poets such as Ernesto Cardenal, who was once a novice at Gethsemani under Merton's tutelage. Whatever Merton knows, he knows through deep reading, reflection, and encounters with particular individuals with whom he develops relationships and friendships. He practises the theology of encounter.

As Robert Inchausti suggests in *Thomas Merton's American Prophecy*, Merton, in a radically pluralistic and fragmented world, "had begun the difficult task of uniting within himself all the various strands of a truly universal Catholicism...through an existential appropriation of the experiential wisdom of many different people."[107] His knowledge is relational, personal, and experiential; it grows by encounter.

For Merton, friendship and relationship are the highest forms of knowing. He seems to know intuitively that we are all made larger by our friends. We become human by our relationships. Words – their parsing, their interpretations, their histories – often divide, while friendships overcome the narcissism of small differences. Merton revels in the title of Rabbi Jonathan Sacks' book *The Dignity of Difference*, and enjoys what each person brings to the human mélange.

Three important encounters in Merton's life occur in the mid-to-late 1960s. He meets in succession three wise men from the East: D.T. Suzuki, an authority on Zen Buddhism; Thich Nhat Hanh, a Vietnamese poet-monk and peace activist; and His Holiness the 14th Dalai Lama, Tenzin Gyatso, from the Tibetan Buddhist tradition. Merton listens, shares, and connects. He develops relationships, even friendships, with all three men. He meets them physically, personally, as body, not as spirit. In the words of the French philosopher Maurice Merleau-Ponty, "Other human beings are never pure spirit for me: I only know them through their glances, their gestures, their speech – in other words, through their bodies."[108]

D.T. Suzuki (1870-1966)

Merton's extended conversation with D.T. Suzuki takes place over two days, June 15 and 16, 1964, in New York City, during one of Merton's rare excursions beyond Gethsemani. Suzuki is 94 at the time; he is frail and hard of hearing. Merton is 49, energetic, and very happy to be back in the city of his college years. Out of their New York encounter comes the dialogue of *Zen and the Birds of Appetite*, a book to which Suzuki himself contributes inspiration and has a small hand in the making. Prior to their meeting, Suzuki had called one of Merton's essays on

Zen, "...one of the best things on Zen to have been written in the West."[109]

Merton's recounting of the meeting with Suzuki goes like this: "I saw Dr. Suzuki only in two brief visits and I did not feel I ought to waste time exploring abstract, doctrinal explanations of his tradition... One cannot understand Buddhism until one meets it in this existential manner, in a person in whom it is alive."[110] The last sentence needs to be repeated and reflected upon. When Merton practises the theology of encounter, he encounters an idea or a particular system of thought existentially, "in a person in whom it is alive." In the intimacy of such encounters, doctrine and abstract differences fall away. What matters is personal connection.

Biographer Michael Mott renders Merton's New York experience vividly in a few novelistic strokes.

> In his room he meditated, sitting on the floor in the position he had first taken up long ago in the apartment at Perry Street... He said Mass, unassisted and unknown, early on two mornings at Corpus Christi, awed by his return to the church where he had been baptized. There were two long talks with Suzuki. Merton found Mihoko Okamura [Suzuki's secretary] charming, and she made green tea for the two monks, who sat together on the sofa. Merton drank from the dark brown earthenware bowl in three and a half sips, as he knew it was done.[111]

The details are significant. They sit together on the sofa, they drink tea together, they drink it in a particular ritualistic manner. Suzuki's last words in summing up are: "The most important thing is Love."[112]

Before meeting Suzuki in the flesh, Merton, seldom sycophantic with those whom he respected, gently chides him in a December 12, 1961 letter to the poet Lawrence Ferlinghetti. He notes Suzuki's tendency at times to fall into the style of thought he so often criticizes: dualistic thinking.

> ...his lineup of Buddha vs. Christ is also dualistic, and when he starts that he forgets his Zen. So he forgets his Zen. He can forget his Zen too if he wants to or has to, no law saying you have to remember your Zen every minute of the day. It seems to me the Cross says just as much about Zen, or just as little, as the serene face of the Buddha."[113]

Out of good manners, Merton may not have brought this difference to Suzuki's attention in New York, but there is no reason to believe that Merton had abandoned it. Differences no doubt remained, as they do in *Zen and the Birds of Appetite*, but the differences narrowed as the friendship deepened.

Thich Nhat Hanh (b. 1926)

Merton's meeting with poet-monk Thich Nhat Hanh takes place in Gethsemani on May 28, 1966. Thich Nhat Hanh is 40 at the time, Merton 52. The young man-older man dynamic is reversed this time.

Nhat Hanh begins his memory of their encounter by remembering the warmth of Merton's face. The physical takes precedence over the spiritual; flesh speaks more loudly than ideas.

> It is hard to describe his face...there was a lot of human warmth – *chaleur humaine* – in him. And conversation with him was so easy. When we talked, I told him a few things, and he understood the things I didn't tell him... He was open to everything... He did not talk so much about himself. He was constantly asking questions. And then he would listen.[114]

Again the details are worth dwelling on. Merton is open. He doesn't talk much. He asks questions. He listens. Nhat Hanh tells Merton a few things which he presumably understands, but he also understands "the things I didn't tell him." Nhat Hanh doesn't elaborate on what those things were, but clearly he gives the reader the sense that their communication was not merely an exchange of language. The word communion may more accurately describe their encounter than the word communication.

Following that meeting, Merton pens a tribute to his new friend, entitled "Nhat Hanh is My Brother." In it, Merton recognizes their common ground – they are both poets, existentialists, and critics of war and oppression. Knowing that the Vietnamese Nhat Hanh would be in danger with the warring factions if he were to return to Vietnam, Merton ends his tribute with, "... Do what you can for him. If I mean something to you, then let me put it this way: do for Nhat Hanh whatever you would do for me if I were in his position. In many ways I wish I were."[115]

He projects himself into Nhat Hanh by saying "do for Nhat Hanh whatever you would do for me if I were in his position."

The Dalai Lama (b. 1935)

Merton has three meetings with the third wise man from the East, the Dalai Lama, in Dharmsala, India, enroute to his talk in Bangkok. The meetings take place in November, 1968. The Dalai Lama is 33 at the time, Merton 53. He is in the role of the older man once again. From the three meetings, a friendship develops: the monk from the West with the monk from the East, the monk from the tradition of Sakyamuni with the monk from the traditions of St. Benedict and the Desert Fathers.

Like Thich Nhat Hanh, the Dalai Lama remarks first on Merton's face. He makes a physical connection.

I looked into his face. I could see a good human being. I don't know how to explain but...you can tell people who

have some deep experience... Honest. Truthful. He was very
open-minded... Yes, we were very serious in our discussions,
but our nature, laughing, joking, teasing quickly came
through... I got a certain feeling I was with a person who
had a great desire to learn...When I think or feel something
Christian, immediately his picture, his vision, his face comes
to me."[116]

The Dalai Lama sees in Merton a like-minded person full of
playfulness, mischief, jest, and profound seriousness. When the
Dalai Lama visits the United States in 1999, he specifically re-
quests to visit Gethsemani and Merton's gravesite.

Merton describes the encounter with the Dalai Lama in *The
Asian Journal* by recounting the succession of meetings. After
the November 4 meeting, he records these words: "The Dalai
Lama is most impressive as a person. He is strong and alert,
bigger than I expected (for some reason I thought he would be
small). A very solid, energetic, generous, and warm person..."[117]

Significantly, Merton begins where the Dalai Lama begins –
with the body. He appreciates the body before moving onto the
mind and the spirit. Both men inhabit Merleau-Ponty's wisdom:
" I only know them through their glances, their gestures, their
speech...through their bodies." Merton and the Dalai Lama get
to know each other through glances, gestures, speech – the body.

At their November 6 meeting, Merton touches on the Dalai
Lama's practical thinking.

It was a very lively conversation and I think we all enjoyed it.
He certainly seemed to. I like the solidity of the Dalai Lama's
ideas. He is a very consecutive thinker and moves from step
to step. His ideas of the interior life are built on very solid
foundations and on a real awareness of practical
problems.[118]

The Dalai Lama remarks on the jokes and teases. Merton stresses the liveliness and joy of the conversation. They choose different words, but their meanings are the same.

By the third and last meeting on November 8 it is clear that Merton feels that he has made a friend.

> It was a very warm and cordial discussion and at the end I felt we had become very good friends and were somehow quite close to one another. I feel a great respect and fondness for him as a person and believe, too, that there is a real spiritual bond between us.[119]

Years later, when remembering Merton for Paul Wilkes' book, the Dalai Lama called Merton a Catholic *Geshe*, a scholar or learned one who is also holy in the sense that he implements what he knows with simplicity, honesty, and respect. Tellingly, the Dalai Lama acknowledges that when Merton died he felt that he had lost one of his best friends.

How does one move from being a stranger to being a friend in the space of three meetings? The Czech novelist Milan Kundera speaks of "a spark" or "a lightning flash" in an encounter of a short duration.[120] Clearly Merton shared a reciprocal spark in his meetings with those three scholars of Buddhism. There is also an element of mystery here. I accept that in a short time Merton could embrace a stranger as a brother in the case of Nhat Hanh, and a stranger as a friend in the case of the Dalai Lama. How that happens I don't know, but it is possible to isolate a few features of Merton's theology of encounter.

In all three encounters Merton listens without pre-judgement. He hears, understands, and appreciates what the other communicates. He asks questions. He shares experiences. And then there is something else at work. Even though Merton knows a considerable amount about Buddhism, he comes to the encounter as a beginner. And somehow, out of listening, questioning, and sharing as a beginner, Merton develops a relationship, which leads to a friendship with the other. The theology of encounter leads to the theology of kindness and respect. Clearly Merton personally likes the three Buddhists whom he encounters; he enjoys their company. He and they belong to different traditions, but they draw from a common source of wisdom and discipline.

P FOR PRAYER

Prayer is the most intimate expression of the human heart. Prayer holds the heart's longings and fears, its wonder and thankfulness. When other forms of speech end, prayer begins. Prayer displays a degree of human vulnerability and self-revelation unequalled in human discourse, even that of a child speaking to a mother. It's as if one is speaking to one's own soul, the deepest and most fragile part of oneself.

Poems manipulate words. Prayers don't need words. The most beautiful mass I ever experienced occurred in Olean, New York, at a St. Bonaventure University Merton Conference on June 25, 1995. It consisted of two young girls solemnly but joyously dancing. That was prayer.

Sometimes prayers are cries, deep sounds, prostrations, gestures of the hands or arms, inner thoughts, wishes for calm, or hopes for peace. Poems are usually polished. Prayers don't need to be. They can be the first and only drafts of an utterance. Prayers can contain only one word, as in Ziggy Marley's song "Justice."[121]

P is a very fertile letter for Thomas Merton. I've already suggested that praise, poetry, and prayer are at the heart of his work. Then you think of P for photography and politics, philosophy and polemics. I've chosen "P for Prayer" because prayer was at the monastic centre of Merton's life and his best poems are in themselves a kind of prayer, as in these lines from an untitled poem to M. that recognize the interconnectedness and interdependency of all people.

No one ever got born
All by himself: It takes more than one.
Every birthday
Has its own theology.[122]

You could ignite a new political movement with these lines. They point to a kind of equality based on the interdependence of each on all. They deflate the myth of self-sufficiency and the self-made individual.

You find prayer everywhere in Merton, even in the most unexpected places. James W. Douglass, in his foreword to *Cold War Letters*, remarks that "Merton knew prayer takes many forms...his *Cold War Letters* were a form of praying in darkness, a search for light with the companions he addressed, in a night of the spirit when everything seemed lost."[123] In a December 15, 1961 letter to Rabbi Zalman Schachter, Merton writes, "And in the political dark I light small, frail lights about peace and hold them up in the whirlwind."[124]

You find prayer in the playful anti-letters with Lax on the death of their friend, abstract expressionist Ad Reinhardt. Reinhardt was noted for his blue-black paintings, where sometimes an almost invisible cross has a powerful presence.

Tomorrow the solemns. The requiems alone in the hermit
hatch. Before the ikons the offering. The oblations. The
clean oblations all round thunder quiet silence black
picture oblations. Make Mass beautiful like big black
picture speaking requiem. Tears in the shadows of hermit
hatch requiems blue black tone. Sorrows for Ad in the
oblation quiet peace request rest... Just old black quiet
requiems in hermit hatch with decent sorrows good by
college chum.[125]

You also see a call, if not to prayer, then to quiet reflection, in Merton's photography, calligraphies and brush drawings.

In *New Seeds of Contemplation*, Merton explores the nature of "mental prayer" (his phrasing) in his typically inclusive manner, where meditation, contemplation, and liturgical prayer merge as one.

> Learn how to meditate on paper. Drawing and writing are forms of meditation. Learn how to contemplate works of art. Learn how to pray in the streets or in the country. Know how to meditate not only when you have a book in your hand but when you are waiting for a bus or riding in a train. Above all, enter into the Church's liturgy and make the liturgical cycle part of your life – let its rhythm work its way into your body and soul.[126]

As frequently happens when reading Merton, you're not sure if he's talking to himself or to the reader – or, as is likely the case, to both at the same time. What strikes me here is how broad Merton's vision of prayer is – how it encompasses writing and reading, making art and looking at art.

Prayer is at the centre of Merton's rich interior life. In "Harpo's Progress," Robert Lax rhetorically asks, "How did his work relate to his prayer?" He answers, "The work took its rise from prayer and returned to prayer. The work itself was prayer and was informed by prayer."[127] Merton's calligraphies and photographs, for instance, were often visual prayers.

Praise and thanksgiving, central and undergirding aspects of prayer, are embedded in church liturgies throughout the world. And they were embedded in Merton's daily liturgies in the Psalms. In his journal entry of May 20, 1961, Merton charges the living world with the imperative to praise.

Today, Father, this blue sky praises you. The delicate green
and orange flowers of the tulip poplar praise you. The
distant hills praise you, with the sweet smelling air that is
full of brilliant light. The bickering fly-catchers praise you,
with the lowing bulls and the quails that whistle over there,
and I too, Father, praise you, with these creatures my
brothers. You have made us all together and you have
placed me here this morning in the midst of them. And here
I am.[128]

With praise comes thanksgiving. In the words of the medieval
Christian mystic Meister Eckhart, whose *Sermons* Merton regarded as one of the most influential books in his early intellectual and spiritual development, "If the only prayer you said in
your whole life was, 'Thank you,' that would suffice."[129]

A one-word prayer of thanksgiving – *merci, gracias* – is immensely powerful. The way the English language says thanks is
with two words. Thank you. There is always someone you thank;
there's always a "you" being addressed. My grandson's prayer, at
age four, lingers with me. At the dining room table in Toronto
some years ago, he said simply, "Thank you, Lord, for my grandparents coming to see me, and thank you for my daddy coming
home safely."

Notably, Merton's critique of the irreligious mind is that it
lacks gratitude for the earth and its incomprehensible gifts of
sustenance and beauty. "Gratitude," says Merton in *Thoughts in
Solitude*, is "the heart of the solitary life, as it is the heart of the
Christian life."[130] When faced with such overwhelming gift as
life itself, what can I do in return other than give thanks.

Sometimes my thanks and prayers take the form of simple
receptivity. Reading lines from Lax's *21 Pages* or Merton's "Hagia
Sophia" while listening to Arvo Pärt's *Spiegel Im Spiegel* while
looking at pictures of Sarah Hall's catacomb windows in
Scarborough, Ontario, I wait for what speaks to me. For me,

prayer is paying homage to the mystery that opens and closes your days.

Perhaps some of the strongest prayers are utterances that are not intended as prayers – what the poet Denise Levertov (another friend of Merton's) calls "oblique prayers," the title of one of her last books. I'm drawn to Thomas Merton's casual, unexpected, oblique prayer about the day:

> It is enough to be, in an ordinary human mode, with one's hunger and sleep, one's cold and warmth, rising and going to bed. Putting on blankets and taking them off, making coffee and then drinking it. Defrosting the refrigerator, reading, meditating, working, praying. I live as my ancestors have lived on this earth, until eventually I die. Amen.[131]

With Merton, prayer is as natural as the cat's purr. "How I pray is breathe," he says in *Day of a Stranger*. "The solitary life is above all a life of prayer," he writes in *Thoughts in Solitude.*[132]

I'm reading the poems of Edward Hirsch at the moment. They sometimes read like prayers. I would venture that Merton would be as enthusiastic about Hirsch's poetry as I am, particularly the extended poem entitled "Earthly Light – Homage to the Seventeenth Century Dutch Painters."

When I read the poem, I think of Vermeer in particular. His scenes of domestic life seem so real and personal it's as if the viewer interrupts a real event: a woman playing a guitar, a woman reading a letter, a woman holding a balance, a woman pouring milk. In each of the 30 or so paintings by Vermeer, the viewer feels privileged to glimpse the beauty and grace of feminine hands at work on small daily tasks. Vermeer's oils are relatively tiny: *Girl with a Pearl Earring* is 18 inches by 15 inches; *Girl with the Red Hat* is slightly more than nine by seven inches. Most would fit in your briefcase or in your carry-on luggage.

Here's Hirsch on Vermeer and other 17th-century Dutch painters:

> ...the Dutch artists prayed obliquely
> by turning away from the other world
> and detailing the plenitude of this.

That plenitude expresses itself in

> the daily pleasures and sufferings
> of usual people, the Saturday nights
> and Sunday mornings of human life.

These oblique and painted prayers lead us back to the dignity of our everyday existence

> because this world, too, needs our unmixed
> attention, because it is not heaven
> but earth that needs us, because
> it is only earth – limited, sensuous
> earth that is so fleeting, so real.[133]

These last lines make me cry. The beauty of the world is so overwhelmingly present in every budding flower, in every fox's run, how can you not cry? And when the earth faces severe climatic spasms with unforeseen consequences, how can you not cry? Love calls us to protect the natural world, to preserve it, to praise it, and to pass it on.

B FOR BEGINNER

"One cannot begin to face the real difficulties of the life of prayer and meditation unless one is first perfectly content to be a beginner... [L]et us be convinced of the fact that we will never be anything else but beginners, all our life."[134]

Merton lived these two sentences in his studies of Zen, in his readings of Latin American poetry, and in his photography and calligraphy. He entered whatever experience presented to him with enthusiasm. He incarnated the attitude that no matter how much prior knowledge he might have, he knew himself to be a beginner.

Merton's appeal for many readers – and his strongest appeal for me personally – has to do with his beginner's approach. He comes at life as if he were a stranger to it and is slowly finding his way in it for the first time. So often he ventures forth, hits a road block, and then regroups. He starts over. He begins again. In his all-too-short life, he enfleshes a code articulated by the folksinger Bob Dylan, whom he enjoyed listening to at the hermitage: "That he not busy being born is busy dying."[135] Merton was always busy being born.

Well-read in the poetry of Rilke, Merton may have internalized some of Rilke's famous lines about being a beginner. Was he familiar with Rilke's lines from "Notes on the Melody of Things"?

> I can imagine no knowledge holier
> than this:
> that you must become one who begins[136]

Very likely. He may also have been familiar with Rilke's letter to Merline on November 18, 1920. "If the Angel deigns to come, it will be because you have convinced her, not by tears, but by your humble resolve to be always beginning; to be a beginner."[137] To be a beginner – *ein Anfanger zu sein*. What a glorious state of mind and heart to be in, to be open to the world, to be Adam once more in the Garden.

When one is a beginner, one waits expectantly, as a groom awaits his bride. Were Merton alive, what would he think of Mary Oliver's Rilkean lines?

...all my life
I was a bride married to amazement.
I was the bridegroom, taking the world into my arms.[138]

The lines are true of Merton's life and of his writing.

So often, Merton writes as if he were seeing something for the first time. You see this habit on display in the journals, particularly in *Turning Toward the World*, when he comments afresh on nature. "An indigo bunting flies down and grasps the long, swinging stem of a tiger lily and reaches out, from them, to eat the dry seed on top of a stalk of grass. A Chinese painting."[139]

How like Merton to move from nature to art, and how like him to integrate them. How like him to be attentive to details – not a bird but an indigo bunting, not a flower but a tiger lily. When you name the world, you must have the right word for each precious part of it. Poet Don McKay says you need acts of close attention to tell one bird from another, one tree bark from another. "It is acts of close attention, such as noticing how the horned larks lower their 'horns' when they run (they never hop like robins or crows) that foster intimacy."[140] Merton fosters intimacy with his precision.

In *Turning Toward the World*, Merton constructs sentences worthy of Thoreau.

A very small gold-winged moth came and settled on the back of my hand, and sat there, so light I could not feel it. I wondered at the beauty and delicacy of this being – so perfectly made, with mottled golden wings. So perfect. I wonder if there is even a name for it. I never saw such a thing before. It would not go away until, needing my hand, I blew it lightly into the woods."[141]

He was alive in, and alert to, nature in all its seasons and expressions. Zorba-like, he cleaved to Wallace Stevens' great line, "The greatest poverty is not to live / In a physical world..."[142]

Sensitivity to nature and gratitude for it are constants in Merton's life. He's always aware of what the weather's doing, how the day is, where the birds and butterflies are. He loves the natural world and the human world that is part of it. He celebrates the day and his immersion in it.

> [W]e have a deep and legitimate need to know in our entire being what the day is like, to see it and feel it, to know the sky is grey, paler in the south, with patches of blue in the southwest, with snow on the ground, the thermometer at 18, and cold wind making your ears ache. I have a real need to know these things because I myself am part of the weather and part of the climate and part of the place, and a day in which I have not shared truly in all this is no day at all.[143]

He dances into a field of thought opened by his friend Thich Nhat Hanh's concept of "interbeing," a concept that explores how each of us is an interdependent part of everything around us.

In Merton's work, you're implicitly invited to be a beginner alongside him. I hear his invitation. I accept it. I want to begin again with my reading and re-reading of Merton. I want to experience afresh his leaps and connections and syntheses.

Merton leans into the world in a distinctive manner, with a beginner's attitude. You see it in *Opening the Bible*, a work composed hurriedly toward the end of his life and published posthumously. Merton reads scripture as if for the first time, and invites the reader to do the same. He rejects readings that seek to provide rescue from the world. The scripture he chooses leads one to a greater immersion in the world. He neither domesticates its wildness nor familiarizes its strangeness. "It is of the very nature of the Bible to affront, perplex and astonish the human mind. Hence the reader who opens the Bible must be prepared for disorientation, confusion, incomprehension, perhaps outrage."[144]

Merton resists the temptation to harden its fluid complexities into rigid dogmas as he explores this "dangerous" (his word) book. He makes reading scripture strange again, allowing himself to be read and questioned by the very book he is reading and questioning. In this dialectic, he reads with the assistance of a Jew (Erich Fromm), a Protestant (Dietrich Bonhoeffer, with additional assistance from Protestant theologians Karl Barth and Rudolf Bultmann), a novelist (William Faulkner), and an atheist (Pier Paolo Pasolini).

A fascinating aspect of Merton's fresh reading of the Bible is his moving encounter with the film "The Gospel According to St. Matthew" by the Italian Marxist poet and filmmaker Pasolini.

> The Christ of Pasolini, young, dark, splendidly aloof, dreadfully serious, was obviously not the sweet, indulgent Jesus of late nineteenth-century Church art. And the apostles were obviously not unreal, shadowy ghosts incapable of understanding a single fact about human existence. These were very real, gnarled, tough men, weather-beaten people who had lived through cruel wars, who had hidden in the mountains from the political police, who knew what the inside of prisons and concentration camps looked like – in a word, they resembled the actual men Christ chose for his disciples![145]

The film has Pasolini himself as St. Peter and his mother as the Virgin Mary. The cast "were not professional actors, but just people – most of them poor and some of them Communists." Merton believed that "the director and the actors had all personally *discovered* the Gospel of Matthew in making the film."[146]

The Bible provokes, disturbs, and challenges. It's a dangerous book, or rather, a dangerous sequence of books. It shocks, jolts, and changes people. One of the ways in which it brings about change in readers is to immerse them in a gripping narrative or a series of events or happenings; lives speak to lives, people speak to people. And for Christians, the central life that speaks most powerfully is the coming of Christ.

"The fullness of the Bible is, then (for Christians), the personal encounter with Christ Jesus in which one recognizes him as 'the one who is sent' (the Messiah or anointed Lord, *Kyrios Christos*)." Merton continues, "The great question of the New Testament, the question which includes all others, is who is Christ, and what does it mean to encounter him?"[147]

The question I've been asking myself for the purpose of this monograph is, *Who is Thomas Merton and what does it mean to encounter him?* A part of one's encounter with him is to engage with an accomplished beginner and to adopt his beginners' outlook on the world.

Merton was, I believe, beginning once again in his last months and days as he was writing *The Asian Journal.* He was making new discoveries about himself. He copies into his notebook a remarkable sentence from Anaïs Nin's short story "The All-Seeing," from *Under a Glass Bell*, a book he was reading on his travels.

> ... the roving gaze of the mariner who never attaches
> himself to what he sees, whose very glance is roving,
> floating, sailing on, who looks at every person and object
> with a sense of the enormous space around them, with a
> sense of the distance one can put between oneself and one's
> desires, the sense of the enormousness of the world and of
> the tides and currents that carry us onward.[148]

I think that this sentence speaks to Merton's desire to be less heatedly involved in personal matters (M.) and politics; it also embodies the essence of the Buddhist principle of non-attachment, which for years I've confused with detachment.

There is an echo of Nin's sentence in *The Asian Journal* when Merton quotes T.R.V. Murti's *The Central Philosophy of Buddhism*. "The essence of the Madhyamika attitude... consists in not allowing oneself to be entangled in views and theories, but just to observe the nature of things without standpoints."[149] Merton was, I think, moving toward non-attachment. And that's how I'd like to move as well in the time given to me. The human world is important, but there are other worlds too.

Toward the end of his life, Merton draws near to Kazantzakis' words in *Zorba the Greek*: "I felt deep within me that the highest point a man can attain is not Knowledge, or Virtue, or Goodness, or Victory, but something even greater, more heroic and more despairing: Sacred Awe!" He seems at last capable of posing Kazantzakis' revolutionary question: "...does our unquenchable desire for immortality spring, not from the fact that we are mortal, but from the fact that during the short span of our life we are in the service of something immortal?"[150] He is ready to serve. He is ready to begin.

1   Thomas Merton, *The Other Side of the Mountain: The End of the Journey. The Journals of Thomas Merton Volume Seven 1967-1968*, ed. Patrick Hart, O.C.S.O. (San Francisco: HarperSanFrancisco, 1998), 237.

2   J.S. Porter, *The Thomas Merton Poems* (Goderich, Ontario: Moonstone Press, 1988), 68.

3   Pope Francis, Address to Congress, www.vox.com/2015/9/24/9391549/pope-remarks-full-text

4   Michael W. Higgins, *The Unquiet Monk: Merton's Questing Faith* (Toronto: Novalis, 2015), 105.

5   Thomas Merton, *The Hidden Ground of Love: Letters on Religious Experience and Social Concerns*, selected and edited by William H. Shannon (New York: Farrar, Straus and Giroux, 1985), 156.

6   Thomas Merton, *Turning Toward the World: The Journals of Thomas Merton Volume Four 1960-1963*, ed. Victor A. Kramer (San Francisco: HarperSanFrancisco, 1997), 59.

7   Thomas Merton, *The Courage for Truth: Letters to Writers*, selected and edited by Christine M. Bochen (New York: Farrar, Straus and Giroux, 1993), 295.

8 Robert Lax, "Harpo's Progress," *The Merton Annual: Studies in Thomas Merton, Religion, Culture, Literature & Social Concerns*, vol. 1 (New York: AMS Press, Inc., 1988), 37.

9 Thomas Merton, *Learning to Love: The Journals of Thomas Merton Volume Six 1966-1967*, ed. Christine M. Bochen (San Francisco: HarperSanFrancisco, 1998), 330.

10 Brother Patrick Hart online interview with Sister Mary Margaret Funk conducted on December 6, 2004: <http://mid.nonprofitoffice.com/index.asp?Type=B_BASIC&SEC...F5AC4F91...Accessed&pri=0&tri=342&pri=0&tri=362> Accessed March 30, 2016.

11 Thomas Merton, *A Search for Solitude: The Journals of Thomas Merton Volume Three 1952-1960*, ed. Lawrence S. Cunningham (San Francisco: HarperSanFrancisco, 1996), 370.

12 Michael Mott, *The Seven Mountains of Thomas Merton* (Boston: Houghton Mifflin Company, 1984), 477.

13 Guy Davenport, quoted in Ralph Eugene Meatyard, *Father Louie: Photographs of Thomas Merton*, ed. Barry Magrid (New York: Timken, 1991), 34.

14 Roger Lipsey, *Angelic Mistakes: The Art of Thomas Merton* (Boston: New Seeds, 2006), 19.

15 Thomas Merton, *Thoughts in Solitude* (New York: Farrar, Straus and Giroux, 1996), 27.

16 Robert Lax, "Remembering Merton & New York" *The Merton Annual*, vol. 5, eds. Robert Daggy et al (New York: AMS Press, Inc., 1997), 55.

17 Robert Lax, *Journal C* (Zurich: Pendo Verlag, 1990), 42.

18 Ron Seitz, *Song for Nobody: A Memory Vision of Thomas Merton* (Liguori, Missouri: Triumph Books, 1993), 34.

19 Robert Lax, "Harpo's Progress," 49.

20 Thomas Merton, *Love and Living*, eds. Naomi Burton Stone and Brother Patrick Hart (San Diego: Harcourt Brace & Company, 1979), 11.

21 Nikos Kazantzakis, *Zorba the Greek* (London: Faber and Faber, 1961), 72-73.

22 Thomas Merton, *Run to the Mountain: The Journals of Thomas Merton, Volume One 1939-1941* (San Francisco: HarperSanFrancisco, 1995), 250.

23 Thomas Merton, *No Man Is an Island* (New York: Harcourt, Brace, 1967), 148.

24 Thomas Merton, *Asian Journal* (New York: New Directions, 1973), 333.

25 Czeslaw Milosz, quoted in Seamus Heaney's *Station Island* (London: Faber and Faber, 1984), 16.

26 Jim Forest, *Living with Wisdom: A Life of Thomas Merton* (Maryknoll, New York: Orbis Books, 1991), xii.

27 Tomas Tranströmer, as quoted in *The Half-Finished Heaven: The Best Poems of Tomas Tranströmer*, selected and translated by Robert Bly (Minneapolis: Graywolf Press, 2001), 60.

28 Thomas Merton, *Dancing in the Water of Life: The Journals of Thomas Merton Volume Five 1963-1965* (San Francisco: HarperSanFrancisco, 1998), 67.

29 Robert Lax, as quoted in James Harford, *Merton & Friends: A Joint Biography of Thomas Merton, Robert Lax, and Edward Rice* (New York: Continuum, 2006), 260.

30 Michael N. McGregor, *Pure Act: The Uncommon Life of Robert Lax* (New York, Fordham University Press, 2015), 18.

31 Robert Lax, *Journal C*, 66.

32 Robert Lax, "Remembering Merton & New York," 52.

33 Robert Lax, as quoted in *Merton By Those Who Knew Him Best*, ed. Paul Wilkes (San Francisco: Harper & Row, 1984), 65.

34 Thomas Merton, *The Courage for Truth: Letters to Writers*, 87.

35 Doris Lessing, *A Small Personal Voice*, <www.dorislessing.org/a.html> Accessed January 25, 2018.

36 Thomas Merton, *Day of a Stranger*, Introduction by Robert E. Daggy (Salt Lake City: Gibbs M. Smith, 1981), 29.

37 Ibid., 53.

38 Ibid., 63.

39 Ibid., 43.

40 Ibid., 43, 45.

41 Ibid., 49.

42 Ernest Hemingway, <http://www.profilesinhistory.com/flipbooks/Historical_84/files/basic-html/page84.html> Accessed January 27, 2018.

43 Thomas Merton, *Learning to Love*, 206.

44 Walt Whitman, "Song of the Open Road," *Leaves of Grass*, Introduction by Gay Wilson Allen (New York: New American Library, 1980), 144.

45 J.S. Porter, *Thomas Merton: Hermit at the Heart of Things* (Toronto: Novalis, 2008), 173.

46 Thomas Merton, "Preface to the Japanese Edition of *The Seven Storey Mountain*," *Introductions East & West: The Foreign Prefaces of Thomas Merton*, ed. Robert E. Daggy (Oakville, Ontario: Mosaic Press, 1981), 47.

47 Thomas Merton, *In the Dark Before Dawn: New Selected Poems of Thomas Merton*, ed. Lynn R. Szabo (New York: New Directions, 2005), 216.

48 Ibid., 149.

49 Ralph Waldo Emerson, *Nature and Selected Essays*, Edited with an Introduction by Larzer Ziff (London: Penguin, 2003), 325.

50 Thomas Merton, *Contemplation in a World of Action* (Garden City, New York: Doubleday/Image, 1973), 160.

51 Thomas Merton, *The Seven Storey Mountain*, (New York: Harcourt Brace Jovanovich, 1978), 3.

52 Thomas Merton, *New Seeds of Contemplation* (New York: New Directions, 1972), 14.

53 Thomas Merton, *A Search for Solitude*, 217.

54 John Berger, *Keeping a Rendezvous* (New York: Pantheon Books, 1991), 47.

55 Thomas Merton, *Run to the Mountain*, 57.

56 Thomas Merton, *Turning to the World*, 151.

57 Thomas Merton, *Dancing in the Water of Life*, 291.

58 Thomas Merton, *Learning to Love*, xxi.

59 Ross Labrie, *The Art of Thomas Merton* (Fort Worth: Texas Christian University Press, 1979), 53.

60 James Harford, *Merton and Friends: A Joint Biography of Thomas Merton, Robert Lax, and Edward Rice* (New York: Continuum, 2001), 207.

61 Merton, *A Search for Solitude*, 45.

62 Thomas Merton, *The Asian Journal of Thomas Merton*, eds. Naomi Burton Stone, Patrick Hart and James Laughlin (New York: New Directions, 1973), 107.

63 Merton, *Asian Journal*, 91.

64 Ibid., 27.

65 Monica Furlong, *Merton: A Biography* (Glasgow: Collins, 1980), 5-6.

66 Merton, *Learning to Love*, 369.

67 Merton, *Run to the Mountain*, 118.

68 Merton, *The Sign of Jonas*, 207.

69 Ibid., 234.

70 Merton, *Run to the Mountain*, 92-93.

71 Ralph Waldo Emerson, *Emerson in His Journals*, Selected and edited by Joel Porte (Cambridge, Mass.: Belknap/Harvard University Press, 1982), 250.

72 Susan McCaslin, editor, *A Matter of Spirit: Recovery of the Sacred in Contemporary Canadian Poetry* (Victoria, B.C.: Ekstasis, 1998), 13.

73 Merton, *Learning to Love*, 353.

74 Merton, *The Sign of Jonas*, 241.

75 Merton, *The Courage for Truth*, 230.

76 Merton, *Turning Toward the World*, 346.

77 Merton, *The Courage for Truth*, 225.

78 Merton, *Run to the Mountain*, 83.

79 Thomas Merton, *The Secular Journal*, (New York: Farrar, Straus & Giroux, 1959), 24.

80 Thomas Merton, *The Literary Essays of Thomas Merton*, ed. Brother Patrick Hart (New York: New Directions, 1981), 128.

81 Merton, *The Courage for Truth*, 166.

82 Malgorzata Poks, "Encounter in a Secret Country: Thomas Merton and Jorge Carrera Andrade," *The Merton Annual*, vol. 18, eds. Victor A. Kramer and David Belcastro (Louisville KY: Fons Vitae, 2005), 140.

83 Merton, *In the Dark Before Dawn*, 37-38.

84 Pete Seeger, "Turn Turn Turn," < http://www.lyricsmode.com/lyrics/p/ pete_seeger/turn_turn_turn.html>. Accessed February 15, 2018.

85 Virginia Woolf, <therumpus.net/2012/perceptive-and-prophetic>. Accessed February 15, 2018.

86 Merton, *The Hidden Ground of Love*, 140.

87 Merton, *Love and Living*, 27.

88 Merton, *Learning to Love*, 84.

89 Merton, *Love and Living*, 27, 35.

90 William Shannon, *Silent Lamp: The Thomas Merton Story* (New York: Crossroad, 1992).

91 Thomas Merton as quoted in James W. Douglass, *JFK and the Unspeakable: Why He Died and Why It Matters* (Maryknoll, New York: Orbis Books, 2008), 11.

92 Ibid., 18.

93 Merton, *Turning Toward the World*, 160.

94 Edward Rice, "Portrait of Thomas Merton" <www.therealmerton.com>. Accessed February 16, 2018.

95 Edward Rice, *The Man in the Sycamore Tree: The Good Times and Hard Life of Thomas Merton* (Garden City, New York: Doubleday/Image, 1972), 152.

96 Merton, *A Search for Solitude*, 168.

97 Stefan Baciu, "The Literary Catalyst," *Continuum. In Memoriam of Thomas Merton*. Volume Seven, Number Two (Summer 1969): 363-365.

98 Robert E. Daggy, Introduction to *Day of a Stranger*, 13.

99 Thomas Merton, *Introductions East & West: The Foreign Prefaces of Thomas Merton*, Foreword Harry James Cargas, Introduction Robert E. Daggy (Oakville, Ontario: Mosaic Press, 1981), 35.

100 Ernesto Cardenal, as quoted in *The Gospel in Art by the Peasants of Solentiname*, eds. Philip and Sally Scharper, (Maryknoll, New York: Orbis Books, 1994), 46.

101 Thomas Merton, *Opening the Bible*, with an Introduction by Rob Stone (Collegeville, Minnesota: The Liturgical Press, 1970), 51.

102 Thomas Merton, *The Collected Poems of Thomas Merton* (New York: New Directions, 1980), 951.

103 Merton, *The Courage for Truth*, 173.

104 Merton, *The Collected Poems*, 944-945.

105 Merton, *Dancing in the Water of Life*, 267.

106 Mary Oliver, "Poem," *Dream Work* (New York: Atlantic Monthly Press, 1986), 52.

107 Robert Inchausti, *Thomas Merton's American Prophecy* (Albany, New York: State University of New York Press, 1998), 128.

108 Maurice Merleau-Ponty, *The World of Perception*, trans. Oliver Davis (London: Routledge, 2004), 62.

109 D.T. Suzuki, quoted by Michael Mott in *The Seven Mountains of Thomas Merton*, 399.

110 Thomas Merton, *Zen and the Birds of Appetite* (New York: New Directions, 1968), 62.

111 Mott, *The Seven Mountains of Thomas Merton*, 399.

112 D.T. Suzuki, quoted in *The Seven Mountains of Thomas Merton*, 399.

113 Merton, *The Courage for Truth*, 271.

114 Thich Nhat Hanh, quoted in *Merton By Those Who Knew Him Best*, 151.

115 Merton, quoted in *The Seven Mountains of Merton*, 455.

116 The Dalai Lama, quoted in *Merton By Those Who Knew Him*, 145.

117 Merton, *The Asian Journal*, 100-101.

118 Ibid., 113.

119 Ibid., 125.

120 Milan Kundera, *Encounter*, trans. Linda Asher (New York: Harper, 2008), 84.

121 Ziggy Marley, "Justice," <http://www.melodymakers.com/music/songs/ songs.cgi?justice>. Accessed February 19, 2018.

122 Merton, "Untitled Poem," *In the Dark Before Dawn*, 194.

123 James W. Douglass, Foreword, *Cold War Letters by Thomas Merton*, edited by Christine M. Bochen and William H. Shannon (Maryknoll, New York: Orbis Books, 2006), xvi.

124 Merton, *The Hidden Ground of Love*, 534.

125 Thomas Merton and Robert Lax, *A Catch of Anti-Letters*, (Sheed and Ward, 1994), 120.

126 Merton, *New Seeds of Contemplation*, 216.

127 Lax, "Harpo's Progress," 37.

128 Merton, *Turning Toward the World*, 120.

129 Meister Eckhart, The Gratitude Prayer, <https://www.goodreads.com/author/ quotes/73092.Meister_Eckhart>. Accessed February 19, 2018.

130 Merton, *Thoughts in Solitude*, 105.

131 Merton, quoted in John Howard Griffin, *Follow the Ecstasy: Thomas Merton, The Hermitage Years, 1965-1968* (Fort Worth, Texas: JHG Editions/Latitudes Press, 1983), 37-38.

132 Merton, *Thoughts in Solitude*, 104.

133 Edward Hirsch, *The Living Fire: New and Selected Poems 1975-2010* (New York: Alfred A. Knopf, 2013), 129, 135.

134 Thomas Merton, *Contemplative Prayer* (Garden City, New York: Doubleday/ Image, 1971), 37.

135 Bob Dylan, "It's Alright, Ma (I'm Only Bleeding)" <www.bobdylan.com/songs/ its-alright-ma-im-only-bleeding>. Accessed February 19, 2018.

136 Rainer Maria Rilke & Maurice Betz, *Rilke in Paris*, trans. Will Stone (London: Hesperus Press, 2010), 87.

137 Rilke, *Selected Poems*, Translated with an Introduction by J.B. Leishman (London: Penguin, 1964) 21.

138 Mary Oliver, *New and Selected Poems*, 10.

139 Merton, *Turning Toward the World*, 228.

140 Don McKay, *The Shell of the Tortoise* (Kentville, Nova Scotia: Gaspereau Press, 2011), 50.

141 Merton, *Turning Toward the World*, 328.

142 Wallace Stevens, *The Collected Poems* (New York: Vintage Books/Random, 1982), 325.

143 Merton, *Turning Toward the World*, 299-300.

144 Merton, *Opening the Bible*, 11.

145 Ibid., 40.

146 Ibid., 41.

147 Ibid., 79.

148 Anaïs Nin quoted by Thomas Merton in *The Asian Journal*, 151.

149 T.R.V. Murti in *The Asian Journal*, 137.

150 Nikos Kazantzakis, *Zorba the Greek*, 273-275.

3

The Divine and Embodied Feminine
A Dialogue

SUSAN MCCASLIN & J.S. PORTER

In the end, it's the reality of personal relationships that saves everything.
— Thomas Merton, from a letter to Jim Forest, February 21, 1966

When you have once seen the glow of happiness on the face of a beloved person, you know that [you] can have no other vocation than to awaken that light on the faces surrounding him...
— Albert Camus, quoted by Thomas Merton, journal entry, Oct. 16, 1966

JSP: In some of your pieces, you seem concerned with how the archetypal feminine relates to the human and personal feminine in Merton's life and works. Why is this so important?

SM: Merton's writings and life as a monk can be interpreted as a flight from the world (*fuga mundi*), especially when that interpretation is based on his spiritual autobiography *The Seven Storey Mountain* (1948). Yet we see him growing increasingly committed to social and political engagement from the late 1950s until his

95

death. His ambivalent memories of his mother, Ruth, who died when he was only six years old, and his anguish at not being able to see her when she was dying of cancer, may have led him to experience her death as abandonment, and perhaps even abandonment by the feminine. In a letter to the young, emerging feminist theologian Rosemary Radford Ruether (March 25, 1967), he implies he had been afraid of rejection by intellectual women. He also notes in his journals around the time of his affair with the young student nurse he called M., that his relationships with women as a young man at Cambridge had been at best superficial and at worst damaging to both parties. One thinks of the young woman he is known to have impregnated during his time at Cambridge. It is interesting that he reflects regretfully on his youthful relationships with women in the journal he wrote during and immediately following the time he was seeing Margie.

JSP: I sometimes think that of all the seismic cataclysms in his life – call them revelations or epiphanies if you prefer – the spasm that hit him hardest wasn't on a Louisville street corner or among the statues in Polonnaruwa. It was his encounter with a particular woman whom we call M. When I think of Tom and Margie, I think of the Stanley Kunitz poem "Touch Me" and these specific lines:

> What makes the engine go?
> Desire, desire, desire.
> The longing for the dance
> stirs in the buried life.
> One season only,
> and it's done.

And it really was one season – one glorious-rich-confusing-turbulent-magical summer. And he's able to get it all down, all his anguish and his love, the way only an artist can. In his *Midsum-*

mer Diary for M., he comes to two shattering realizations. One, that "[l]ucidity does not prevent anguish," and two, that "I have a rich life, but built on the central cost of cruel deprivation." *Midsummer Diary*, or "the account of how I once again became untouchable," is a significant document on love, but it has one large weakness. It's primarily a monologue rather than a dialogue. The *Diary* is missing M.'s views, although she is present in the journal at large. He quotes her: "The happiest I have ever been is when I took care of you in the hospital... Being without you isn't the hardest thing – it's not being able to give you anything except thoughts and prayers... You keep me, you guard me, you protect me in all my ways." You can see by her words what Merton meant to her. I sometimes mischievously think that I ought to work on a poem called "Margie's reply to Tom" and have as my opening lines,

> You became untouchable;
> I became untouched.
> Your condition was chosen;
> mine was imposed.

When Merton chose the spiritual path over the family path, he made a decision that greatly affected them both. In *Thoughts on Solitude*, Merton recognizes that "[t]he spiritual life is first of all a life. It is not merely something to be known and studied, it is to be lived." You can't be a monk and be married. You'd end up not doing justice to either life. You can hear the pain in Merton's voice. "I do not know how on earth I am going to live without ever seeing you, talking to you, being with you, loving you warmly and directly, pressing you to myself and kissing you. It will have to be, but I do not know how it is going to be, or how I am going to stand it." And you can hear the pain implied in M.'s voice. "Will we ever see each other again?... What will I do without you?... How unfair it is, even inhuman..."

SM: What you say about Merton's relationship with Margie being a "seismic cataclysm" certainly expresses my sense of the importance of this relationship, John. My sense is it wasn't until he stumbled into this messy, painful affair that he opened fully to the depths of human love with a living woman. As Michael Mott points out in his seminal biography *The Seven Mountains of Thomas Merton* (1984), after Margie, Merton "never again talked of his inability to love, or to be loved."

Certainly his post-conversion experiences of the feminine drew him into the realms of the iconographic, historical, biblical, and mystical traditions of Catholicism. His early monastic life, with its honouring of the sacred figures of Mary, our Lady of Cobre in Cuba, and Thérèse of Lisieux, his patron saint, allowed Merton to express his reverence for sacred images of the divine feminine. From the time of his conversion to Catholicism, he embraced archetypal icons of female saints and delved into studies of mystics like Teresa of Avila and Catherine of Siena. In *Mystics and Zen Masters* (1961), he calls the 14th-century English mystic Julian of Norwich "the greatest of all English mystics."

Despite this adoration of the archetypal divine feminine in the first half of his life, he mostly lacked the opportunity to interact intimately with a broad range of living, breathing women. He did develop meaningful friendships with his agent and editor Naomi Burton Stone, his friend Tommie O'Callaghan, and his trusted friend, editor, and assistant Sister Thérèse Lentfoehr. He respected and admired Raissa Maritan, the wife of his correspondent and friend, philosopher Jacques Maritain. Yet it's interesting that toward the end of his life he was reading psychiatrist Karl Stern's *The Flight from Woman*, which explores the polarity of the sexes as a damaging socially constructed division.

JSP: When you say that Merton's experience with women tended to be with nuns and editors and female correspondents, you take me back to his first words about M. "M. is terribly inflammable, and beautiful, and is no nun, and so tragically full of passion and so wide open." He knew from the start that she was a woman who was fully alive. They didn't stay together long enough to reach and overcome Leonard Cohen's lines in "Democracy" about

> the homicidal bitchin'
> that goes down in every kitchen
> to determine who will serve and who will eat.

Yet they are together long enough to reveal their own and see each other's naked souls.

I agree with you on the importance of elevating the feminine principle to divinity, and so did Carl Jung. Jung regarded the papal proclamation of Mary's Assumption by the Catholic Church in 1950 as "the most important religious event since the Reformation." The affirmation of God as Mother as well as Father is enormously important. The difficulty I have is that we don't yet have a full enough image of the Feminine. The image needs to include the wild woman, the laughing woman, the working woman, the kick-ass woman, and so on, along with the woman as nurturer, life-bearer, and care-giver. With M., Merton experienced a woman in the flesh, not a woman you pray to or read about or give talks on. M. was a woman with real needs and demands. He comes as close to a balanced view of womanhood as his short years would allow him. The recent biography of James Laughlin, Merton's friend and publisher, makes clear that Laughlin reaches out to Margie shortly after Merton's death to reassure her that Merton had fully sensed the depth of her devotion to him. "It seems clear to me that he did understand, and that you were as close to him as any mortal person could be."

After his experience with M., Merton writes the very beautiful "Love and Need: Is Love a Package or a Message?" The piece, from the posthumous collection of essays entitled *Love and Living*, is still somewhat idealistic, but it includes a very down-to-earth view of the process of falling in love. "If you don't look where you are going, you are liable to land in it [water]: the experience will normally be slightly ridiculous. Your friends will all find it funny...." To fall in love is to risk making a fool of yourself, whether you're Thomas Merton or you or me.

SM: I like what you're saying about these fuller, richer, less stereotypical aspects of what society has constructed as the feminine, John. I'm remembering how in the late 50s to early 60s, during which time Merton was experiencing a series of visionary dreams of Proverb or the Hebrew figure of Wisdom (1958), studying the Eastern Orthodox sophianic mystical traditions (1958-59), and publishing "Hagia Sophia," he began to awake to the wilder, less passive, feminine divine within himself and others. It's interesting to me that Proverb, the biblical figure of divine Wisdom, comes to him in dreams as an intense, young, Jewish woman who clings to him. In this context, she is certainly not a passive figure. For me, the trajectory of Merton's last decade is a steady turning to Proverb-Sophia as the active embodiment of the inclusive divine feminine in each of us. She, like the Hindu Shakti and the Jewish Kabbalistic Shekinah, is also the creative, active power of God immanent in the world. She comes to him not merely as the female face of a masculine God, but as creative Presence, an embodied power within what he calls God. She is God, but she is also one of the many names and images of the God beyond all concepts and names.

After this time Merton turns more to active engagement with living women. Though he had developed friendships with strong women such as the Baroness Catherine De Hueck Doherty at Friendship House, and Dorothy Day, the founder of the Catholic Worker Movement, he comes now to study sophianic mystical traditions and interact with strong, creative, intellectually challenging women like Joan Baez, Denise Levertov, Mary Luke Tobin, and Rosemary Ruether.

JSP: A few notes on your women, Susan. Dorothy Day was a pivotal friend in encouraging the redirection of his political thinking from bystander to writer-activist. His August 21, 1961 letter to Day announces his decision to address for the first time "life-and-death issues" of war and peace. He sends her his famous article "The Root of War is Fear," he writes for *The Catholic Worker*, he begins *The Cold War Letters,* and so on. They have enormous respect for each other. And I think Merton has a sense that she is the one in the combat zone fighting for the poor and the broken, while he is more of a commentator. They never met in person but they met on paper, and what a beautiful correspondence they had.

Levertov, as you know, wrote two poems inspired by Merton's dreams. Who's lucky enough to get his dream life put into poems by a great poet?

The feisty correspondence with Ruether is like nothing else he engaged in. I met her once at a weekend retreat. She was tremendously energetic and intellectually stimulating. She shook some of Merton's intellectual foundations just as M. shook his emotional foundations. Tobin I heard speak about Merton very warmly and affectionately at the Louisville Conference in 1988, the first international gathering of Merton scholars and enthusiasts. She spoke to the audience as if she had lost her brother.

Then there's Baez. My wife and I were privileged to hear Baez twice, once in Lewiston, New York, and once at the University of Toronto. All through his relationship with M., Merton played Baez's song "Silver Dagger" at the hermitage. She wrote the song "Gethsemani's Bells" after reading Tom's elegy on the death of his brother. Imagine how thrilling it was for the aging monk when he opened his door one morning and looked into the eyes of the young, beautiful, and immensely gifted Joan Baez. Wow! Merton must have felt that he had died and gone to straight to heaven. In his journal Merton wrote of the experience of entertaining her at the hermitage, where she sat on the rug "eating goat-milk cheese and bread and honey and drinking tea, in front of the fire." He describes her as a "precious, authentic, totally human person...a kind of mixture of frailty and indestructibility."

Clearly the encounter was of importance to Baez as well. She wrote about it in her autobiography and in *Merton: By Those Who Knew Him Best*. She writes, "The time I spent with Martin Luther King was laughing. I mean, we just laughed. That's how you survive. And the time I spent with Thomas Merton, we mostly laughed. It was very important, life-sustaining."

SM: I'm glad you mentioned these creative and dynamic women with whom Merton shared laughter, John. When I met Rosemary Ruether at a Merton conference at the Vancouver School of Theology (July 2007), we had an amicable chat on the balcony of the Iona Building overlooking the beautiful coastal mountains of British Columbia. I found her refreshingly unwilling to buy into a certain kind of hagiography that can sometimes surround Merton. She still refuses to be a "Merton fan," and I admire her for that. When she first corresponded with Merton (August 1966–February 1968), he was defending the kind of patriarchal monasticism that she, as a young feminist, was radically questioning. She was in favour of more direct social and political engagement. By dialoguing with her on such issues he demonstrated his openness to what was to become second wave feminism.

A few months before his correspondence with Ruether,

Merton met Margie, a young student nurse, while in hospital for back surgery. Her relationship to him as his nurse seemed uncannily foreshadowed by sections of "Hagia Sophia." In the poem, Sophia-Wisdom arouses him from sleep in the figure of a nurse. Four years later, he and Margie had the turbulent, life-changing love affair you so eloquently described. Although one can be cynical about his affair with Margie due to the discrepancy of their ages and the obvious power imbalance, I feel it wasn't until he entered stumblingly into this messy, painful affair that he opened fully to the depths of human love with a woman.

JSP: Messy, yes. The human is messy. No messiness, no humanity. Bob Marley sings, "No Woman, No Cry." If I could sing, I'd sing, "No Mess, No Human."

I find your words so intriguing, Susan, about how Merton seems to foretell his own future. He dreams of a nurse with "a soft voice," who awakens him out of "languor and darkness, out of helplessness... / In the cool hand of the nurse there is the touch of all life, the touch of Spirit." I love that conjoining of flesh and spirit, or Spirit – so very Mertonian. And that's what happens, isn't it? The poetic meditation takes on flesh a few years after the writing of it. He finds himself in a hospital, he meets a nurse, and she really does wake him up, and lift him up – for a time anyway. And amen to your, "he opened fully to the depths of human love with a woman."

SM: Yes, Margie seems to have cracked Tom wide open. Some might argue that Merton, while moving out of patriarchal structures, still falls at times into gender stereotypes, assigning the soft, gentle, and passive to the feminine and the strong, assertive, and active to the masculine. In "Hagia Sophia," the voice of Sophia-Wisdom is maternal in many ways, which indeed she is. But looking more deeply, it is she who also plays the role of the "awakener" who arouses the male figure representing humanity and the *Logos* (Merton the speaker and the Word) from sleep; so in many ways she is an active, creative power in the world. In this poem, and in his living out its implications with the various women in his life, including Margie, he wrestles with apparent oppositions in himself, the world, and within the divine, and seeks the "polarity within unity" which his early hero William Blake called "the contraries." Marion Woodman, the Jungian feminist writer, writes of the integration of masculine/feminine characteristics within each of us. In opening to various kinds of intimacies with women, Merton was opening to the deep feminine within himself, which is part of an enfolding, an indwelling, a flow, rather than a set of binaries.

JSP: Let me be personal here. I bristle when people associate gentleness and tenderness exclusively with the feminine. In my own case, whatever I learned about being gentle and tender I learned from my father. My mother has these qualities too, but I didn't learn them from her. From my mother, I think I learned a degree of clear-sightedness and a lack of sentimentality – toughness, in a word. From the masculine, I received the gift of the feminine, and from the feminine the gift of the masculine. Go figure.

SM: In my family of origin this was the case as well. My father was the nurturer, the quieter, gentler spirit, while my mother was more outspoken, spirited, creative, and assertive. In "Hagia Sophia," Merton does present the feminine as gentleness. Yet her peace is an active, creative power that also embodies a compelling energy, a vital force something like what Gandhi calls "soul power" or *Satyagraha*. Gender has a biological basis, but is also culturally constructed, not only in the West but worldwide. Therefore, many people still tend to see men and women in terms of these stereotypes.

At a retreat with the Sisters of Loretto in 1967, not long before Merton leaves for his final Asian tour, he engages with a group of nuns at a neighbouring convent. During that time together they touch on the controversy surrounding Betty Friedan's best-selling book *The Feminine Mystique* (first published 1963). Merton is quick to embrace Friedan's argument that the construction of women as sweet, mild, subordinate man-pleasers is destructive to both men and women alike. He also references Mary Daly, the radical feminist theologian, who goes on to write *Beyond God the Father* (1973). Merton paraphrases what Mary Daly had argued, "that, in one and the same breath, women are idealized and humiliated by it [the mystique]. This mystique is an instrument of oppression for women." He proceeds to urge the Sisters to assert themselves against the oppression of their male superiors by simply going ahead with what they must do and say without always asking permission, which is exactly what Mary Luke Tobin, Merton's long-time friend, went on to do after his death. She participated as a witness at the Second Vatican Council, supported women's ordination, opposed nuclear proliferation, challenged the unsustainable practices of the Blue Diamond Coal Company, took part in nonviolent demonstrations at a nuclear weapons plant, danced, and founded a Buddhist-Christian dialogue/meditation group.

In the last decade of his life, Merton seems to be moving toward ever-fuller integration with self, nature, and humanity, living out the new gender equality not merely through theology or ideology, but through intimate encounter. What strikes me most is that his affirmations of the need for solitude and the need for community aren't contradictory, but two parts of a vital whole. Solitude *and* community. Retreat to the silent, inner ground of being *and* attention to our essential interconnectedness in the public realm. My hunch is that at the end of his life he experienced a conjunction of that yin and yang in himself. The feminine for Merton is gentle, soft, fierce, strong, wild, and evolutionary. Although he lived and wrote before LGBT issues came to the fore, his concept of God transcends and includes the many nuances of gender. His God is masculine, feminine, liminal, androgynous, and mysterious beyond all our constructed categories.

JSP: Yes. Beautifully put. "His God is masculine, feminine, and mysterious beyond all our constructed categories." There's much I'm in sync with. I note your choice of words, however: "moving toward even fuller human integration..." Merton was moving toward integration, but I'm not sure he or anyone else fully achieves it. I'm not even sure it would be desirable to achieve it. Closing time, methinks...You might as well die. Nothing remains to be struggled with. You only get to live one life. You can only combine a certain number of things. Merton brought his poetry, his spirituality, and his politics into integration, it seems to me. The richness of experiencing another human being over time in its fullness was not a part of his life. He has some lacks, like the rest of us in our broken alphabets. He didn't experience the joy and difficulty of loving a child over a long period of time, for example. To live the life he chose he had to give up some things; he missed out on some things. What happens after his "break-up" with Margie is that he comes to the wisdom that the "I" is such a fragile thing. He becomes acquainted with his own fragility. On September 6, 1966 he writes, "There is 'I' – this patchwork, this bundle of questions and doubts and obsessions, this gravitation to silence and to the woods and to love. This incoherence!!"

The sculptor Stephen De Staebler, a Christian, makes the human patchwork visible. His sculptures often have incongruous bronze-and-clay body parts stuck awkwardly to each other, with bits hanging. There is an unfinished look to his work, a deliberately unintegrated look. If you made a visual for Merton's great sentence on his individual patchwork you'd be looking at a De Staebler sculpture. De Staebler's "outsides" are our "insides."

I love Merton's definition of the "I," Susan. I love his doubts, and questions, and obsessions. I love his marginality and his humanness. His is the very best definition of selfhood I've ever come across, and it would have been impossible without his encounter with M. He must have said prayers at night. Thank you, Lord, for putting that amazing woman on my path.

SM: I have to agree, John, not only with your sense of how M.'s presence led to a breakthrough, but with how you see Merton's doubts and contradictions as a gift. I've written an essay called "The Problem with Perfect," and I love the way your Alphabet acknowledges his (and our) shared frailty, brokenness, and incompleteness as held within a larger wholeness. Merton's humanity and how he expresses, embraces, and surrenders it – this is what draws you, me, and so many others to him. In the end, his autobiographical writings aren't about Merton the personality so much as about us, his readers, and the liminal spaces between his writings and us. Through his words we are invited to embrace our own whole and broken selves with tenderness. He helps us see our original faces shining mysteriously in and through the imperfect.

When I spoke of him moving toward integration, I didn't have in mind a sense of static arrival, but that he was growing, struggling, evolving rather than attaining "perfection" as an end product. In both Eastern and Western spirituality there is a sense of the spiritual life as growth toward maturity, as continual opening to mystery and greater love. The Dalai Lama calls it enlightenment (waking up), but does not see it as an endgame, a finality. Merton expresses it as discovering within our fragmented selves "a hidden wholeness." Perhaps this state can only be expressed in the poetic language of paradox (as feminist American poet

Marge Piercy does in her poem "I Saw Her Dancing"), since it lies beyond concepts and words.

I Saw Her Dancing

Nothing moves in straight lines
but in arcs, in epicycles, in spirals, in gyres.
Nothing living grows in cubes or cones or rhomboids
but we take a little here and give a little here
and we change
and the wind blows right through us and knocks the apples
from the tree and hangs a red kite suddenly there
and a fox comes to bite the apples curiously
and we change
or die
and then change.
It is many as drops
it is one as rain
and we are in it, in it, of it.
We eat it and it eats us
and fullness is never and now.[1]

Merton expresses something similar at the end of *The Asian Journal*.

In prayer we discover what we already have. You start where
you are and you deepen what you already have, and you
realize that you are already there.

While in Asia, Merton grapples with the mystery of how we are fractured and whole, male and female, multi-gendered and gender-transcendent, in new and deeper ways. In his last journal entries, he writes of the holy mountain of Kanchenjunga.

O Tantric Mother Mountain! Yin-yang palace of opposites in
unity!... The full beauty of the mountain is not seen until
you too consent to the impossible paradox: it is and is not.
When nothing more needs to be said, the smoke of ideas
clears, the mountain is SEEN.

The mountain is both a "mother" and a place where talk of
opposites (mother/father) is held within a wordless mystery. If
gender lies along a finely nuanced spectrum, then what Merton
calls God is both the entirety of that spectrum and that which
holds the masculine and feminine, flesh and spirit, in unitive
being, which lies on a continuum beyond words and concepts.
Because he found and lost and found himself on what has been
called the apophatic way (the way of unknowing where individual consciousness arises from and returns to silence), Merton's
words have the capacity to unify rather than divide.

If you envision a stream or river of multi-coloured light,
then what the West has called "the Godhead" and the East "the
One" is the unsayable mystery from which the colours emerge
and into which they vanish. Or as Leonard Cohen puts it in
"Boogie Street,"

It is in love that we are made
in love we disappear.

1   Marge Piercy, *Available Light: Poems by Marge Piercy* (NY: Knopf, 1988), 121.

4.

Embodying Sophia

SUSAN MCCASLIN

There is in all visible things an invisible fecundity, a dimmed light, a meek namelessness, a hidden wholeness. This mysterious Unity and Integrity is Wisdom.
— Thomas Merton, from "Hagia Sophia"

What healing might arise in our own small circle of the world if we — male and female alike — embodied Sophia more intentionally and fiercely in our various ways, in our families, institutions, and worldly occupations?
— Christopher Pramuk, from *At Play in Creation*

Hagia Sophia
— Thomas Merton (1962)

I. DAWN. THE HOUR OF *LAUDS*

There is in all visible things an invisible fecundity, a dimmed light, a meek namelessness, a hidden wholeness. This mysterious Unity and Integrity is Wisdom, the Mother of all, *Natura naturans*. There is in all things an inexhaustible sweetness and purity, a silence that is a fount of action and joy. It rises up in wordless gentleness and flows out to me from the unseen roots of all created being, welcoming me tenderly, saluting me with indescribable humility. This is at once my own being, my own nature, and the Gift of my Creator's Thought and Art within me, speaking as Hagia Sophia, speaking as my sister, Wisdom.

I am awakened, I am born again at the voice of this my Sister, sent to me from the depths of the divine fecundity.

Let us suppose I am a man lying asleep in a hospital. I am indeed this man lying asleep. It is July the second, the Feast of Our Lady's Visitation. A Feast of Wisdom.

At five-thirty in the morning I am dreaming in a very quiet room when a soft voice awakens me from my dream. I am like all mankind awakening from all the dreams that ever were dreamed in all the nights of the world. It is like the One Christ awakening in all the separate selves that ever were separate and isolated and alone in all the lands of the earth. It is like all minds coming back together into awareness from all distractions, cross-purposes and confusions, into unity of love. It is like the first morning of the world (when Adam, at the sweet voice of Wisdom, awoke from nonentity and knew her), and like the Last Morning of the world when all the fragments of Adam will return from death at the voice of Hagia Sophia, and will know where they stand.

Such is the awakening of one man, one morning, at the voice of a nurse in the hospital. Awakening out of languor and darkness, out of helplessness, out of sleep, newly confronting reality and finding it to be gentleness.

It is like being awakened by Eve. It is like being awakened by the Blessed Virgin. It is like coming forth from primordial nothingness and standing in clarity, in Paradise.

In the cool hand of the nurse there is the touch of all life, the touch of Spirit.

Thus Wisdom cries out to all who will hear (*Sapientia clamitat in plateis*) and she cries out particularly to the little, to the ignorant, and the helpless.

Who is more little, who is more poor than the helpless man who lies asleep in his bed without awareness and without defense? Who is more trusting than he who must entrust himself each night to sleep? What is the reward of his trust? Gentleness comes to him when he is most helpless and awakens him, refreshed, beginning to be made whole. Love takes him by the hand, and opens to him the doors of another life, another day.

(But he who has defended himself, fought for himself in sickness, planned for himself, guarded himself, loved himself alone, and watched over his own life all night, is killed at last by exhaustion. For him there is no newness. Everything is stale and old.)

When the helpless one awakens strong at the voice of mercy, it is as if Life his Sister, as if the Blessed Virgin, (his own flesh, his own sister), as if Nature made wise by God's Art and Incarnation were to stand over him and invite him with unutterable sweetness to be awake and to live. This is what it means to recognize Hagia Sophia.

II. EARLY MORNING. THE HOUR OF *PRIME*

O blessed, silent one, who speaks everywhere!

We do not hear the soft voice, the gentle voice, the merciful and feminine.

We do not hear mercy, or yielding love, or non-resistance, or non-reprisal. In her there are no reasons and no answers. Yet she is the candor of God's light, the expression of His simplicity.

We do not hear the uncomplaining pardon that bows down the innocent visages of flowers to the dewy earth. We do not see the Child who is prisoner in all the people, and who says nothing. She smiles, for though they have bound her, she cannot be a prisoner. Not that she is strong, or clever, but simply that she does not understand imprisonment.

The helpless one, abandoned to sweet sleep, him the gentle one will awake: Sophia.

All that is sweet in her tenderness will speak to him on all sides in everything, without ceasing, and he will never be the same again. He will have awakened not to conquest and dark pleasure but to the impeccable pure simplicity of One consciousness in all and through all: one Wisdom, one Child, one Meaning, one Sister.

The stars rejoice in their setting, and in the rising of the Sun. The heavenly lights rejoice in the going forth of one man to make a new world in the morning, because he has come out of the confused primordial dark night into consciousness. He has expressed the clear silence of Sophia in his own heart. He has become eternal.

III. HIGH MORNING. THE HOUR OF *TIERCE*

The Sun burns in the sky like the Face of God, but we do not know his countenance as terrible. His light is diffused in the air and the light of God is diffused by Hagia Sophia.

We do not see the Blinding One in black emptiness. He speaks to us gently in ten thousand things, in which His light is one fulness and one Wisdom.

Thus He shines not on them but from within them. Such is the loving-kindness of Wisdom.

All the perfections of created things are also in God; and therefore He is at once Father and Mother. As Father He stands in solitary might surrounded by darkness. As Mother His shining is diffused, embracing all His creatures with merciful tenderness and light. The Diffuse Shining of God is Hagia Sophia. We call her His "glory." In Sophia His power is experienced only as mercy and as love.

(When the recluses of fourteenth-century England heard their Church Bells and looked out upon the wolds and fens under a kind sky, they spoke in their hearts to "Jesus our Mother." It was Sophia that had awakened in their childlike hearts.)

Perhaps in a certain very primitive aspect Sophia is the unknown, the dark, the nameless *Ousia*. Perhaps she is even the Divine Nature, One in Father, Son, and Holy Ghost. And perhaps

114

she is in infinite light unmanifest, not even waiting to be known as Light. This I do not know. Out of the silence Light is spoken. We do not hear it or see it until it is spoken.

In the Nameless Beginning, without Beginning, was the Light. We have not seen this Beginning. I do not know where she is, in this Beginning. I do not speak of her as a Beginning, but as a manifestation.

Now the Wisdom of God, Sophia, comes forth, reaching from "end to end mightily." She wills to be also the unseen pivot of all nature, the center and significance of all the light that is in all and for all. That which is poorest and humblest, that which is most hidden in all things is nevertheless most obvious in them, and quite manifest, for it is their own self that stands before us, naked and without care.

Sophia, the feminine child, is playing in the world, obvious and unseen, playing at all times before the Creator. Her delights are to be with the children of men. She is their sister. The core of life that exists in all things is tenderness, mercy, virginity, the Light, the Life considered as passive, as received, as given, as taken, as inexhaustibly renewed by the Gift of God. Sophia is Gift, is Spirit, *Donum Dei*. She is God-given and God Himself as Gift. God as all, and God reduced to Nothing: inexhaustible nothingness. *Exinanivit semetipsum*. Humility as the source of unfailing light.

Hagia Sophia in all things is the Divine Life reflected in them, considered as a spontaneous participation, as their invitation to the Wedding Feast.

Sophia is God's sharing of Himself with creatures. His outpouring, and the Love by which He is given, and known, held and loved.

She is in all things like the air receiving the sunlight. In her they prosper. In her they glorify God. In her they rejoice to reflect Him. In her they are united with him. She is the union between them. She is the Love that unites them. She is life as communion, life as thanksgiving, life as praise, life as festival, life as glory.

Because she receives perfectly there is in her no stain. She is love without blemish, and gratitude without self-complacency. All things praise her by being themselves and by sharing in the Wedding Feast. She is the Bride and the Feast and the Wedding.

The feminine principle in the world is the inexhaustible source of creative realizations of the Father's glory. She is His manifestation in radiant splendor! But she remains unseen, glimpsed only by a few. Sometimes there are none who know her at all.

Sophia is the mercy of God in us. She is the tenderness with which the infinitely mysterious power of pardon turns the darkness of our sins into the light of grace. She is the inexhaustible fountain of kindness, and would almost seem to be, in herself, all mercy. So she does in us a greater work than that of Creation: the work of new being in grace, the work of pardon, the work of transformation from brightness to brightness *tamquam a Domini Spiritu*. She is in us the yielding and tender counterpart of the power, justice, and creative dynamism of the Father.

IV. SUNSET. THE HOUR OF *COMPLINE.*
"*SALVE REGINA.*"

Now the Blessed Virgin Mary is the one created being who enacts and shows forth in her life all that is hidden in Sophia. Because of this she can be said to be a personal manifestation of Sophia, Who in God is *Ousia* rather than Person.

Natura in Mary becomes pure Mother. In her, *Natura* is as she was from the origin from her divine birth. In Mary, *Natura* is all wise and is manifested as an all-prudent, all-loving, all-pure person: not a Creator, and not a Redeemer, but perfect Creature, perfectly Redeemed, the fruit of all God's great power, the perfect expression of wisdom in mercy.

It is she, it is Mary, Sophia, who in sadness and joy, with the full awareness of what she is doing, sets upon the Second Person, the *Logos*, a crown which is His Human Nature. Thus her consent opens the door of created nature, of time, of history, to the Word of God.

God enters into His creation. Through her wise answer, through her obedient understanding, through the sweet yielding consent of Sophia, God enters without publicity into the city of rapacious men.

She crowns Him not with what is glorious, but with what is greater than glory: the one thing greater than glory is weakness, nothingness, poverty.

She sends the infinitely Rich and Powerful One forth as poor and helpless, in His mission of inexpressible mercy, to die for us on the Cross.

The shadows fall. The stars appear. The birds begin to sleep. Night embraces the silent half of the earth. A vagrant, a destitute wanderer with dusty feet, finds his way down a new road. A homeless God, lost in the night, without papers, without identification, without even a number, a frail expendable exile lies down in desolation under the sweet stars of the world and entrusts Himself to sleep.

MERTON AND HAGIA SOPHIA (HOLY WISDOM)

Wisdom will honour you if you embrace her
She will place on your head a fair garland
She will bestow on you a crown of glory.
— Proverbs 4. 8-9

A mysterious figure of Wisdom makes her first appearances in Merton's journals of 1958 as a recurrent dream persona he called "Proverb," based on the figure of Wisdom in Proverbs 8.

When visiting Vienna-born artist, printmaker, and typographer Victor Hammer in Lexington, Kentucky in 1959, Merton

ΑΓΙΑΣΟΦΙΑ

HAGIA SOPHIA

noticed a triptych depicting a dark-haired young woman crowning a youth. Hammer had begun depicting the woman as a Madonna but said he no longer knew exactly who the woman was, as she had turned out quite differently than originally intended. Immediately Merton interjected, "I know who she is. I have always known her. She is Hagia Sophia."[1]

In his scattered journal entries, and especially in the prose poem "Hagia Sophia," completed in the spring of 1961 during Pentecost, Merton explores this ancient feminine figure of God. The poem grew out of a letter Merton wrote in response to Hammer's request for more detail on the identity of Sophia. In "Hagia Sophia," Merton invokes the sophianic character of Eastern Orthodoxy, anticipating later feminist reconfigurations of the divine by embracing a sense of the reciprocity and unity of male and female polarities in God, the world, and the self.

THE IDENTITY OF HAGIA SOPHIA

Merton's letter to Hammer, dated May 2, 1959, develops in more detail the identity of the young Madonna in the triptych.

> The first thing to be said, of course, is that Hagia Sophia is God Himself. God is not only a Father but a Mother. He is both at the same time... [T]o ignore this distinction is to lose touch with the fullness of God. This is a very ancient intuition of reality which goes back to the oldest Oriental thought... For the "masculine-feminine" relationship is basic in all reality – simply because all reality mirrors the reality of God.[2]

The poem "Hagia Sophia" names Wisdom as "the dark, nameless *Ousia* [essence or ground of being] of the Father, the Son, and the Holy Ghost; the 'primordial' darkness which is infinite light;" "the wisdom of God;" "the Tao; the nameless pivot of all being and nature;" "the feminine child playing before God;" "the *mercy* of God;" and "the feminine, dark, yielding, tender counterpart of the power, justice, [and] creative dynamism of the Father."[3]

The poem was printed privately by Hammer in January of 1962 as a limited-edition imprint (Stamperia del Santuccio, Library Press) and reprinted in a second edition with Hammer's icon, based on a woodcut engraving, illustrating the text. The poem appeared in the magazine *Ramparts* in March of 1963 and became finally the centerpiece of Merton's book of poems *Emblems of a Season of Fury* (New Directions, 1963). "Hagia Sophia" was written when Merton was moving from a more parochial sensibility based on a sense of *fuga mundi* to a universal, politically engaged, ecumenical Catholicism in which contemplation enters a dialectic with social action. In this poem he remains within the lyrical-meditative mode, experimenting with the long prose poem, but not yet turning to the "anti-poetry" or more experimental forms of his later years (evidenced in *Cables to the Ace* and *The Geography of Lograire*).

"Hagia Sophia" is an extended poetic meditation on Holy Wisdom. It alternates between a heightened, first-person lyric voice and the tone of a more formal hymn to Wisdom blending private and public utterance. Set in the framework of the canonical hours of monastic prayer, it enacts the daily passage from morning to evening, waking to sleep. Merton has chosen to relate each section to one of the liturgical hours within this span of time: dawn or *Lauds*, early morning or *Prime*, high morning or *Tierce*, and sunset or *Compline* when the "Salve Regina" was sung at Gethsemani. The poem links Sophia to the Eternal Feminine, the cycles of the day, and the cycles of liturgical prayer.

Hagia Sophia, or Holy Wisdom, is invoked through a complex nexus of symbols. She is Wisdom, Sister, Bride, Mother, Nurse, Child, Muse, Lady Poverty (of St. Francis), Eve, Mary (Our Lady, the Blessed Virgin, Incarnation, Virgin), Mercy, Gift (*Donum Dei*), *Ousia*, *Natura Naturans* (creating nature as opposed to created nature or *Natura Naturata*), and the "unseen pivot of all nature."[4] The names are archetypes embedded in the particularity of the poet-speaker's existential situation. Merton foregrounds the gentler qualities associated with woman in many cultures, such as tenderness, receptivity, pardon, grace, peacemaking, and mercy. Yet Sophia is not simply the passive pole of a binary in which Spirit is privileged over matter, male over female, light over darkness, and strength over meekness. She is also a comprehensive and evolving presence best expressed in the mystical language of paradox. She is, for instance, both "God-given and God Himself as Gift" (III, 368). Experiencing her requires an "unknowing" or apophatic approach to language. As Merton puts it in the letter to Hammer, "[T]o arrive at her beauty we must pass through an apparent negation of created beauty"[5] This is so because she is part of the uncreated ground of all Being. She is not merely one Person of a hypostatic union in God (one of the Persons of the Trinity), but the ontological base of all things known and unknown. She is the mystery of the Godhead in both essence and existence, being and becoming. She cannot be known through her names or signs, but only approached through contemplation that moves toward oneness with her. She is the silent centre (pivot) in which the interior self and the Divine Self converge. She is indeed a figure of contemplation. Merton writes in section III,

> Perhaps in a certain very primitive aspect Sophia is the unknown, the dark, the nameless *Ousia*. Perhaps she is even the Divine Nature, One in Father, Son and Holy Ghost. And perhaps she is in infinite light unmanifest, not even waiting to be known as Light.

MERTON'S BIBLICAL AND MYSTICAL SOURCES
FOR "HAGIA SOPHIA"

What is the provenance of this profoundly mysterious figure of whom Merton speaks so tentatively, using the word "perhaps"? His sources include his own interior and psychological awakening to the feminine as charted in his dreams and reflections, the figure of Wisdom in Judeo-Christian Wisdom literature, and the figure of Sophia in 19th-century Eastern Orthodox Russian mystical theology. His primary source, however, is the Wisdom tradition in the Hebrew Bible, allegorized both in Talmudic commentary and in Christianity. The original Hebrew words *Ruah* (Spirit), *Hokhmah* (Wisdom), and *Shekinah* (the female aspect of God) are either feminine or grammatically inclusive of both genders, suggesting what later feminists have seen as a repressed feminine aspect to the Godhead within patriarchal Judaism.

Merton's principal source is Proverbs 8, where Wisdom is personified as a woman standing at a crossroads and calling to humankind to follow her way of justice. She is also portrayed in the Wisdom literature of the Bible as a presence at creation, as God's partner dancing the world into being. As a cosmological presence at creation, she was subsequently associated in the Gospel of John and the Pauline writings with Jesus as the *Logos* or Wisdom of God, similarly co-eternal with God in the beginning. Though Christ as the *Logos* or Word of God is masculine in his incarnation, he has been seen as a son of Wisdom, embodying her values of peace-making and mercy in the world. In the Jewish Wisdom literature, Sophia is linked to both creative power and justice (judgment), and not simply the traditional feminine role of gentle nurturer. Like the Christ as divine *Logos*, she represents God as cosmic Mediator.

Sophia in Merton's poem is also associated with the Bride. Merton was, of course, well-acquainted with the tradition of Christian ecclesiological symbolism, drawn from both the *Song of Songs* and the book of *Revelation*, in which the Church is the Bride of Christ. He had studied the long tradition of patristic commentary on the *Song of Songs* going back to Origen. Allegorically, the female beloved has been interpreted variously as Israel, the Church, and as the soul in union with God. He knew Boethius' famous *Consolation of Philosophy*, which features the figure of Sophia, and would have been familiar with the medieval use of feminine metaphors for God by both male and female monastics of the 11th and 12th centuries. Merton was immersed also in Christian mysticism that took up nuptial symbolism as an expression of the most intimate union of God and the soul, as evidenced by writers such as Bernard of Clairvaux, Catherine of Siena, John of the Cross, and Teresa of Avila.

It's the 14th-century English mystics that figure most prominently in the poem however, particularly Julian of Norwich. In March of 1961, around the time "Hagia Sophia" was written, Merton reflects in his journal that "I am still a 14th-century man: the century of Eckhart, Ruysbroek, Tauler, the English recluses, the author of the Cloud...a lover of the dark cloud in which God is found by love."[6] He alludes parenthetically to the 14th-century mystics in section III of the poem, highlighting the mystical theology of Julian who develops the image of Jesus as Mother in her *Revelations of Divine Love*.

> When the recluses of fourteenth-century England heard their Church Bells and looked out upon the wolds and fens under a kind sky, they spoke in their hearts to "Jesus our Mother." It was Sophia that had awakened in their childlike hearts. (III, 367)

THE RUSSIAN MYSTICAL THEOLOGIANS

Another wellspring for Merton's "Hagia Sophia" is Eastern Orthodoxy, and especially the Russian Orthodox mystical theologians of the 19th and 20th centuries whose theology deeply honoured the divine feminine. Merton's journals indicate he was reading Macarius Bulgakov and Nicholas Berdayev between 1957-1959, a few years prior to writing "Hagia Sophia." He reflects on Bulgakov's sophianism in his journal, Aug. 7, 1957, suggesting that if God as Sophia is immanent in creation, then all of nature is a theophany of God. Matter and spirit, nature and God, immanence and transcendence are not severed. Merton distances himself from the dualism of his youth and moves toward a much more sacramental worldview in which Sophia is that in God which longs for incarnation.

> I think this morning I found the key to Bulgakov's sophianism. His idea is that the Divine Sophia, play, wisdom, is by no means a fourth person or hypostasis, yet in *creation*... hypostasized, so that creation itself becomes the "Glory of God"....[7]

Moving on from his reading of Bulgakov's *The Wisdom of God*, Merton implies that if God is hypostasized (of one substance) with Sophia or the feminine principle in creation, then humankind's posture should not be one of control over nature, but of humility in light of our interconnectedness with her. Humankind's utter dependence on Sophia as Nurse, Mother, Sister, Beloved is indeed the central theme of "Hagia Sophia." Merton reflects in a journal entry of April 25, 1957.

> They [Bulgakov and Berdyaev] have dared to accept the challenge of the sapiential books, the challenge of the image of Proverbs where Wisdom is "playing in the world" before the face of the Creator.[8]

For the Russians, Sophia is God's *Ousia*, the matrix of the three hypostases – the Father, Son, and Spirit. She is the Ground of Being of the created cosmos and the basis of the image of God in creation and humanity. She is humanly manifest in the maternity of Mary the mother of Christ, whose receptivity to God's purpose can only be understood as an expression of Holy Wisdom.[9] In section IV of the poem, Merton celebrates Mary as the earthly medium of the heavenly Sophia. Bulgakov's theory on the close relation between the Blessed Virgin and Sophia brought him under investigation by the Church in 1922 when he was accused of "promulgating the doctrine of an androgynous Christ" and characterizing God equally as 'Father' and 'Mother.'"[10] In exploring the notion that Sophia is a disclosure of God in creation, these theologians were challenging the boundaries of the patriarchal orthodoxy of their times by re-introducing the feminine into an understanding of the Godhead.

Vladimir Soloviev (1853-1900), another Russian mystical theologian Merton was reading around the time of writing, posits that God's other or feminine self is the universe, the world in which Wisdom desires to be incarnate.

> Such a realization and incarnation is also the aspiration of the eternal Femininity itself, which is not merely an inert image in the Divine mind, but a living spiritual being possessed of all the fullness of powers and activities.[11]

Soloviev sees Sophia as a cosmic feminine presence both transcendent and immanent in the world. He suggests that all beings are inwardly both male and female. This implies that God contains a balance of both male and female attributes. Like Soloviev, Merton in "Hagia Sophia" places much emphasis on littleness, meekness, hiddenness, and childlikeness as powerful, transformative qualities in Sophia and in those who incarnate her presence.

The Russian mystical theologian who had the most impact on Merton's thought at this time was Paul Evdokimov (1901-1970), who taught at Saint-Serge in Paris, and wrote *La femme et le salut du monde* (1945) (*Woman and the Salvation of the World*). Merton made a notation in his journal on this book on September 18, 1959 and spent much of his retreat in January of 1960 reading Evdokimov in the original French.[12] Jonathan Montaldo calls this book "required reading...for appreciating the appearance of the dream figure 'Proverb' [Wisdom] in Merton's journals" of 1958 and points to Merton's "copious marginalia" in his copy.[13] Evdokimov was also an expert on Greek Orthodox iconography and took the Orthodox perspective that a sacred ikon can mediate Divine Presence. It is significant that Merton's "Hagia Sophia" grew out of an act of gazing at a sacred image of Holy Wisdom. Through an act of participation in which the image mediates ultimate reality, the viewer may experience the actual presence of the saint, Christ, or, in this case, God revealed as Holy Wisdom.

For Evdokimov, as for Merton in "Hagia Sophia," Mary's virginity is not a sign of her difference from other women or her need for detachment from the "evils" of the flesh, but rather is symbolic of a state of "integrated being" (wholeness) or childlike purity attainable by all. The Greek term *sophronsyne*, meaning "integrity that is in conformity with Wisdom," denotes a state of "ontological chastity."[14] Hagia Sophia is a figure of immense power in Merton's poem precisely because of such ontological purity. She is that which is incorruptible in the human spirit. God's purpose in Eastern Orthodox thought, as Evdokimov characterizes it, is not merely humankind's salvation from the effects of the Fall, but the restoration of the original Divine Image in each person through the Incarnation.[15] Like the *Logos* crowned and sent forth into the world by Mary-Sophia in Merton's poem, each person is born into the world to incarnate the lost or corrupted *Imago Dei*. In Eastern Orthodoxy the deification or *theosis* of humankind is possible through mystical or interior transformation. Evdokimov calls sophiology "the glory of Eastern Orthodoxy" because of its sacramental view of nature, writing that "the inwardness of nature unfolds into the infinite."[16] Sophia is this inward aspect of nature opening into the eternal presence of God.

PSYCHOLOGICAL NEXUS: HAGIA SOPHIA AS MERTON'S FEMININE SELF

Merton's developing sense of an inward feminine principle also suggests a psychological level to the poem, where he embraces the feminine not only theologically but personally. As the son of a mother perceived as strong, distant, and sometimes critical, and who died when he was six, Merton needed to reconnect to the feminine self or *anima* in his own psyche.[17] Yet the poem "Hagia Sophia" is only one stage in a slowly developing trajectory that began as early as his experience of the Virgin in Cuba during Easter Week 1939. This experience is reflected in his early poem, "Song for Our Lady of Cobre," the product of his visit to the Basilica of Our Lady of Cobre as recorded in *The Seven Storey Mountain*.[18]

Wisdom (as Proverb) also figures prominently in Merton's well-known Fourth and Walnut epiphany, described in *Conjectures of a Guilty Bystander* (1965). In this poem he acknowledges himself not as someone set apart because of his religious vocation, but as only a man among others with faces "shining like the sun."[19] In a journal entry of February 29, 1965 that precedes the epiphany by four days, he writes,

> I am embraced with determined and virginal passion by a young Jewish girl. She clings to me and will not let go, and I get to like the idea. I see that she is a nice kid in a plain, sincere sort of way. I reflect, "She belongs to the same race as St. Anne." I ask her name and she says her name is Proverb. I tell her that is a beautiful and significant name, but she does not appear to like it – perhaps the others have mocked her for it.[20]

In his journal, Merton expresses poignantly his sudden sense of profound interconnection with ordinary people on the street (primarily women) and reflects on the nature of this dream figure tied to Saint Anne, the mother of Mary. It is clear from the context of the "letters" to Proverb in his journals preceding and following the well-known epiphany that Proverb is for him a personalized figure of Wisdom. It is significant that his epiphany takes place at the public "crossroads" of Fourth and Walnut in downtown Louisville, for in Proverbs Wisdom cries out to people at the crossways or marketplace of life. It is as if Wisdom herself, in the form of "Proverb," calls Merton, the solitary monk, to a sense of his deep involvement with the world and with women.

> For the woman-ness that is in each of them [each woman he saw on the street] is at once original and inexhaustibly fruitful bringing the image of God into the world. In this each one is Wisdom and Sophia and Our Lady – (my delights are to be with children of men!).[21]

Merton and Karl Stern

A final contribution to Merton's developing sense of involvement with womankind (and with individual women) was his encounter with psychologist Karl Stern, a Jewish convert to Catholicism who visited the monastery in March 1958 and later published a book called *The Flight from Woman* (1965).[22] Stern critiques six Western male writers (Descartes, Goethe, Schopenhauer, Kirkegaard, Tolstoy, and Sartre) for harbouring an almost pathological fear of the feminine, which is expressed both in their writings and in their personal lives. Though Stern sometimes assumes the archetypal feminine to be essentially intuitive rather than analytical, he traces what he sees as an irrational misogyny ingrained in Western culture and suggests that fear-based attitudes toward woman and the earth with which she has been associated have led to the victimization and "colonization" of actual women. He argues that God is the ultimate ground of reciprocity of male and female powers in each person, and that humankind is essentially androgynous in origin and destination. Jonathan Montaldo suggests that Merton's series of dreams of Proverb needs to be read in the context of Merton's exposure to Stern's ideas, since the dreams and correspondence with Stern occur around the same time.[23]

An Exegesis of "Hagia Sophia"

I. DAWN. THE HOUR OF *LAUDS*

This brief survey of Merton's personal and theological sources for "Hagia Sophia" allows for a richer tracing of the layered metaphors for Wisdom that play out in the poem. The *Lauds* section, celebrating the Feast of Our Lady's Visitation (July 2), opens at 5:30 a.m. in a hospital when the speaker awakens to the gentle voice of "Hagia Sophia, speaking as my sister, Wisdom."

> There is in all visible things an invisible fecundity, a dimmed light, a meek namelessness, a hidden wholeness. This mysterious Unity and Integrity is Wisdom, the Mother of all, *natura naturans*. (I, 363)

In July of 1960 Merton was hospitalized for several days. This section is strangely premonitory of Merton's encounter six years later with the student nurse called M. with whom he fell deeply in love. The similarities in the language he uses to describe Sophia and M. certainly seem to suggest a Jungian "synchronicity" in which archetype and reality merge. In Merton's "Midsummer Diaries" (June 23, 1966), where he struggles with his love for M., he speaks of her in the same tone used to describe Proverb-Sophia.

I will never be without the mysterious, transcendent
presence of her essential self that began to speak to me so
. stirringly and so beautifully those early mornings in May
between sleeping and waking. She [M.] will always be to me
her soft voice speaking out of the depths of my own heart
saying that the central reality of all is found in our love that
no one can touch and no one can alter.[24]

"Hagia Sophia" opens in the early morning in a similar hypnogogic state where the soft voice of the Nurse arouses the patient from sleep. This section attempts to answer the question,
"What is it like to awaken to the voice of Wisdom?" Oxymorons
such as "invisible fecundity" and "dimmed light" enable Merton
to suggest that Wisdom is an active power deliberately tem-
pered to meet human limitations. She is God's mercy encoun-
tering our poverty with her own "indescribable humility." The
speaker compares this moment at dawn to humankind stirring
from a dream, Christ awakening in "all the separate selves,"
Adam first hearing the voice of Eve in paradise, and humanity
(Christ) being awakened by the Blessed Virgin. Sophia's power
to quicken through her voice echoes the divine "Fiat" of God at
creation, the calling forth of new life through the Word. Here
Merton may have in mind as well the Kabbalistic myth of "Adam
Kadmon," the primordial man whose fragments are drawn together by the voice of the Shekinah.

It is like the first morning of the world (when Adam, as at
the sweet voice of Wisdom awoke from nonentity and knew
her), and like the Last Morning of the world when all the
fragments of Adam will return from death at the voice of
Hagia Sophia, and will know where they stand. (I, 364)

Sophia is an eschatological presence active at both beginning
and ending – an Alpha and Omega. In Christian typology, of

course, it is common to read Eve as a type or prefiguration of Mary. In the poem, however, Eve, Mary, and Sophia form a kind of Triune Feminine, with Hagia Sophia taking the part of the Holy Spirit as a feminine unifying presence.

It is interesting that the unification of the fragmented human and reintegration of male and female powers in each person through love and "mutual forgiveness" is the central myth of the later works of William Blake, the Romantic poet who most continuously influenced Merton throughout his lifetime. In Blake's mythos, the reunion of male and female counterparts (the Zoas with their feminine Emanations) resolves itself in the final union of Albion with his bride Jerusalem. In this poem, Merton emphasizes the utter dependency of humanity on the feminine for healing through a series of rhetorical questions.

> Who is more little, who is more poor than the helpless man who lies asleep in his bed without awareness and without defence? Who is more trusting than he who must entrust himself each night to sleep? (I, 364)

If Merton's central myth, like that of Blake, is the loss of an original paradisal unity, this is a poem that enacts the possibility of healing (wholeness) through the presence of the feminine.

II. EARLY MORNING. THE HOUR OF *PRIME*

In section II, or *Prime*, the tone shifts from that of a dreamer in the hypnogogic state describing Wisdom in tentative symbols and metaphors to that of prayer-like apostrophe. "Oh blessed, silent one, who speaks everywhere!" The motif of awakening continues, but the tone turns to lament as the poet decries the community's collective rejection of Wisdom. Evdokimov describes this renunciation in terms of the world's "darkening" of the image of Sophia through [hu]man's overthrow of the sacred order.[25] As in Proverbs 8, she cries out at the crossroads, but we seal our ears. Merton uses anaphora (repetition of initial phrases) to grieve this human resistance to Mercy who is, in a lovely turn of phrase, "the candor of God's light."

> We do not hear the soft voice...We do not hear Mercy, or yielding love, or non-reprisal...We do not hear the uncomplaining pardon that bows down the innocent visages of flowers to the dewy earth...We do not see the Child... (II, 365)

Section II is the most lyrical part of the poem. Drawing on the nature personification of the Psalms where setting stars and rising sun rejoice in the cycle of creation, the speaker advances from darkness into the light of consciousness by admitting "the clear silence of Sophia in his own heart" (II, 366). The archetypes of Wisdom in the forms of Mother and Sister modulate into that of the Child as incorruptible innocence. This is not the naïve innocence that refuses experience, but the inviolable purity of utmost interiority. Wisdom here is something like what Merton elsewhere called the *"point vierge"* or virgin centre of the heart.[26] The Child is Wisdom playing before the throne of God in her elements of creativity and spontaneity.

> She [the Child] smiles, for though they have bound her, she cannot be a prisoner. Not that she is strong, or clever, but simply that she does not understand imprisonment. (II, 366)

Having awakened to the "pure simplicity" of Wisdom as the Child, the speaker prepares for the light of the rising sun.

III. HIGH MORNING. THE HOUR OF *TIERCE*
In Section III, *Tierce* or High Morning, the Sun as the "Face of God" is again "diffused" into the softer light of Hagia Sophia that shines from within each individual, and in the created or-

der ("in ten thousand things"). Though Merton accepts as unproblematic the traditional binaries of male and female as direct light versus mediated light, he also emphasizes that God as Sophia is incarnate in creation as Mercy and Tenderness.

> He is at once Father and Mother. As Father He stands in solitary might surrounded by darkness. As Mother His shining is diffused, embracing all His creatures with merciful tenderness and light. The Diffuse Shining of God is Hagia Sophia... In Sophia His power is experienced only as mercy and as love. (III, 367)

A feminist reading of the poem might find the identification of the feminine with mercy and tenderness problematic if doing so restricts the feminine to the "softer" virtues or subordinates the feminine to the masculine in a hierarchical order. Feminist theorists have pointed out how God-language affects the lives of women. However, such subordination of Sophia to a masculine God does not, in fact, occur in the poem, since qualities of tenderness and mercy are also demonstrable in God the Father when united with Sophia. We are told, "He speaks to us gently in ten thousand things..." (III, 366). Also, Sophia exercises power and authority when she crowns the *Logos* and sends him forth into the world in section IV.

Ultimately, Sophia represents the darkness of "unknowing" as well as the dawn light. The metaphors for male and female are interconnected and interchangeable in the poem. God is not simply transcendent and Sophia immanent, or God active and Sophia passive. Gender metaphors are an expression of two aspects of a single dynamic at play, like Wisdom at the foundation of the world.

It is paradoxical that in Section III, which celebrates high morning, Merton's poem turns to metaphors of darkness. The efforts to name Sophia, to catch her in the net of language, defer to the apophatic tradition of "unnaming" (describing something in terms of what it is not, rather than what it is, in order to suggest its ineffability). Every naming becomes an unnaming, a backing off from language, and an insistence that words and names are inadequate before mystery. Sophia herself becomes "the unknown, the dark, the nameless." The "I" speaker summons words to back away from words. "I do not know where she is, in this Beginning. I do not speak of her as a Beginning, but as a manifestation." The entire section moves repeatedly from naming to unnaming. The speaker's struggle with language reminds us that all gender-bound metaphors for ultimate reality are inadequate, since God is not an object of knowledge. The God who is male and female, father and mother, is simultaneously neither male nor female, and transcends gender categories. Because Merton's metaphors move into the mystical language of apophasis or "unsaying," they remain fluid. Sophia is the "nameless *Ousia*," the unmanifest or unknown being of God.

IV. SUNSET. THE HOUR OF *COMPLINE*.
"SALVE REGINA."

In this section, Merton invokes the monks' evening singing of the "Salve Regina" (a Gregorian hymn sung or recited in honour of Mary, Mother of God), and thus Sophia in her manifestation as "the Blessed Virgin Mary." The "Salve Regina" is one of the seasonal antiphons, at the close of which the monks at the Abbey of Gethsemani extinguish all lights in the abbey church except the one directed at the image of the Virgin in a window over the altar."[27] The "Salve Regina" section of Merton's poem ends with the return to sleep and darkness; yet the ending is the beginning of a new cycle in which the Virgin crowns Christ (mankind) and sends him forth into the world (waking). In one of the monographs of "Hagia Sophia" printed by Hammer, Merton placed the following text from Proverbs 4: 8-9, establishing the biblical source for the image.

> Wisdom will honour you if you embrace her. She will place
> on your head a fair garland. She will bestow on you a crown
> of glory."[28]

In "Hagia Sophia," Mary-Sophia, dressed in a simple Greco-Roman robe, crowns Christ as well as the Merton-speaker. She is not portrayed as the mother of an infant or as a royal Queen of Heaven. The poem establishes, through her sending forth of the *Logos* or Son, that we share a common humanity as ones who have undergone birth. As Christ or the *Logos*, the Incarnation of Wisdom, the Child goes forth to His destiny: crucifixion and resurrection. As humanity the child goes forth, an Everyman or Everywoman, into exile from paradise. The conclusion suggests the speaker's sense of his own homelessness, vagrancy, and destitution as well as the position of Christ (born to us and in us) as an Incarnation of Feminine Wisdom. Wisdom's child, like Christ, "has nowhere to lay his or her head." The final passage presents a strangely modern figure of the exile or God as exile in us.

> A vagrant, a destitute wanderer with dusty feet, finds his
> way down a new road. A homeless God, lost in the night,
> without papers, without identification, without even a
> number, a frail expendable exile lies down in desolation
> under the sweet stars of the world and entrusts Himself to
> sleep. (IV, 371)

The image of Sophia or the Divine Feminine crowning the *Logos* is an act of feminine power. The more traditional depictions of "the Coronation of the Virgin" in Christian art show Mary being crowned by Christ rather than actively bestowing the crown upon him. In Hammer's triptych and Merton's poem, the usual relation is inverted so that Sophia's tenderness and gentleness "crowns Him [Christ] not with what is glorious, but with what is greater than glory: the one thing greater than glory is weakness, nothingness, poverty" (IV, 370). In her crowning of Christ with his "human nature," she reminds us that all people come from a common womb (the earth, the Feminine) and are alike in our vulnerability, frailty, and utter dependence on the earth and the feminine matrix. The Christ-like potential in each is crowned (reaches its maturity or fulfillment) through gentleness, tenderness, and compassion. Christ in this depiction is not external to us and apart, but within, poor and homeless in the world. What Wisdom requires is an utter extinguishing of ego, like the nightly entrusting of the self to sleep. The ego must become a nameless "nobody" through whose *kenosis* (self-emptying) Wisdom enters the world.

Merton's Anticipation of Feminist Concerns

Some feminists have expressed concern that the figure of Mary has been used to oppress women by holding up an impossible ideal of woman as both virgin and mother. Feminist theorists of the "liberation theology" schools, however, see Mary as a locus of power for the disempowered because of her willing consent to the purpose of God and because of her "Magnificat." This canticle speaks of a reversal of the positions of oppressors and oppressed when God "[puts] down the mighty from their seats, and [exalts] them of low degree" (Luke 1:52). Merton exalts Mary for her humility and links her to the cosmological creativity of Sophia as an image of the fullness of God.

How gendered metaphors for God are contextualized culturally is significant, and the political and social implications of God-talk are crucial. Certainly, Merton's poetic texts on the feminine divine have to be read within a mystical tradition in which the ground of each person's being is consubstantial with the centre of what has been called God. In this context, Wisdom offers to all a way of becoming divine, or awakening to the divine Wisdom within.

"Hagia Sophia," though employing traditional polarities of male and female, avoids a dualistic framework that subordinates the female to the male or objectifies the feminine. Merton is aware of the radical unconventionality of the poem in terms of its treatment of the feminine. In his journal (July 8, 1962) he writes, "The Hammers were here yesterday. Brought...the little paper of Hagia Sophia... It is pretty, but my theology is strange in it. It needs revision and reformulation."[29] Michael Mott, one of Merton's chief biographers, notes that "Hagia Sophia" was a kind of "secret work," circulated in mimeographed letters primarily to non-monastic artists and friends because it expressed Merton's "deepest and most unorthodox thought."[30]

In what sense is "Hagia Sophia" unorthodox (not right-thinking) in the commonly used sense of the word? Firstly, Merton celebrates the feminine in a culture where the feminine has been feared, denigrated, and suppressed. Secondly, the poem implies that the salvation of humanity through the feminine is due to the values of peace, mercy, and forgiveness that Sophia represents in her expressions of softness, tenderness, and non-retaliation. Merton writes on Evdokimov in his journal:

[T]he icon of wisdom, the dancing ikon – the summit reached by so many non-Christian contemplatives (would that it were reached by a few Christians!) Summit of Vedanta – Faith in Sophia, *Natura naturans*, the great stabilizer today – for peace.[31]

If one looks at the poem "Hagia Sophia" in the context of the book in which it was published, *Emblems of a Season of Fury*, the way in which Sophia calls for the transformation of the world through non-violence and non-retaliation is even more evident.

Many poems about injustice, war, and corruption lead up to and emerge from "Hagia Sophia," including some of Merton's most powerful poems such as "There Has to be a Jail for Ladies," "And the Children of Birmingham," and "Chant to be Used in Procession Around a Site with Furnaces." Of all his books of poetry, *Emblems* is perhaps Merton's best at establishing the inseparability of the socio-political and the spiritual, and striking a balance between his lyrical and ironic (prophetic) voices. Sophia becomes the unifying ground of political action.

As a dissident within a patriarchal structure, Merton revives ancient feminine metaphors for the divine. Though he may be less conscious than later feminist theorists about projecting feminine images of God to correct a perceived imbalance, Merton's "Hagia Sophia," read in the context of his work as a whole, complements the work of later feminists by recovering lost feminine images and voices. Merton is aware that the sapiential (sophiological) tradition had been marginalized within Western Christianity, and he attempts to restore it. Later and more radical forms of feminism have gone further in appropriating methods of deconstruction to destabilize and dismantle naïve forms of essentialism – the association of the feminine with stereotypical qualities. Later feminists would examine how social and linguistic constructions of the feminine affect power relations between men and women and contribute to the oppression of women. If God is idolized as a male authority figure, then women can be excluded from positions of power. In terms of Cartesian dualisms of spirit over matter, transcendence over immanence, and so on, woman has been associated with the flesh, earth, matter (mater), and mothering more than with spirit, power, justice. Some feminists have argued that the emphasis on transcendence as a flight from the body, nature, woman, and the earth has led to a disembodied spirituality and a related devaluation of woman, while ecofeminists tie the devaluation of woman to the devaluation of nature.

Conclusion

Merton's use of feminine metaphors for God in "Hagia Sophia" is part of a long process of development in which he opens himself to the feminine at many levels of being. He is not interested in simply reversing the positions of oppressor and oppressed by replacing "God the Father" with "the Goddess." He uses gendered metaphors interchangeably to suggest a presence and a power beyond gender and beyond gendered binaries. What prevents "Hagia Sophia" from reinforcing gender stereotypes is the way Merton uses metaphors as tentative approximations of a nameless mystery.

In "Hagia Sophia" Merton is a poet intuitively receiving and shaping images and symbols for the divine, rather than a systematic philosopher or theologian. A poem is a play of metaphors and silences rather than a theological construct. Unlike critical theory, or philosophy of religion, his poem does not deconstruct gender paradigms, but makes "old things new" through the transformative power of imagination. While Merton recognizes the limitations of language, he assumes an ontological ground of being beyond language; that is, the "real presence" of Wisdom behind and within the signs.

1   Thomas Merton, *Witness to Freedom: Letters in Times of Crisis*, ed. William H. Shannon (San Diego: Harcourt Brace & Co., 1994) ,3.

2   Ibid., 4.

3   Ibid., 4.

4   Thomas Merton, *The Collected Poems of Thomas Merton* (NY: New Directions, 1977), 363-371. All subsequent references to the poem "Hagia Sophia" will be drawn from this volume and cited by section number and page.

5   Merton, *Witness to Freedom*, 5.

6   Thomas Merton, *Turning Toward the World: The Journals of Thomas Merton*, Vol. 4: 1960-1963, ed. Victor A. Kramer (NY: HarperCollins, 1996), 99.

7   Thomas Merton, *A Search for Solitude: The Journals of Thomas Merton*, Vol. 3: 1952-1960, ed. Lawrence S. Cunningham (San Francisco: HarperCollins, 1996), 107.

8   Merton, *A Search for Solitude*, 86.

9   Rosemary Radford Ruether, *New Woman, New Earth: Sexist Ideologies and Human Liberation* (San Francisco: Harper & Row, 1975), 44-45.

10 Caitlin Matthews, *Sophia, Goddess of Wisdom: the Divine Feminine from Black Goddess to World-Soul* (Hammersmith, London: Mandala Press, 1991), 298-299.

11 Vladimir Solovyov, *The Meaning of Love*, Introd. Owen Barfield (Hudson, NY: Lindisfarne Press, first translated 1945; 1985), 92-93.

12 Michael Mott, *The Seven Mountains of Thomas Merton* (Boston: Houghton Mifflin, 1984), 138.

13 Jonathan Montaldo, "A Gallery of Women's Faces," in *The Merton Annual*, Vol. 14 (Sheffield Academic Press, 2001), 156.

14 Paul Evdokimov, *Woman and the Salvation of the World: A Christian Anthropology on the Charisms of Women*, translated Anthony P. Gythiel (Crestwood, NY: St. Vladimir's Seminary Press, 1994), 217.

15 Ibid., 72-73.

16 Ibid., 66-67.

17 Robert G. Waldron, *Thomas Merton in Search of His Soul: A Jungian Perspective* (Notre Dame, Indiana: Ave Maria Press, 1994).

18 Thomas Merton, *The Seven Storey Mountain* (NY: Harcourt, Brace & Co., 1948), 281-282.

19 Thomas Merton, *Conjectures of a Guilty Bystander* (NY: Doubleday & Co., 1968), 157.

20 Merton, *A Search for Solitude*, 176.

21 Ibid., 182.

22 Karl Stern, *The Flight from Woman* (NY: Farrar, Straus & Giroux, 1965).

23 Montaldo, "A Gallery of Women's Faces," 156-157.

24 Thomas Merton, *Learning to Love (Volume VI): Exploring Solitude and Freedom, 1966-1967*, ed. Christine Bochan (NY: HarperCollins, 1997), 336.

25 Evdokimov, *Woman and the Salvation of the World*, 66.

26 Merton, *Conjectures of a Guilty Bystander*, 158. Merton derived this phrase from the scholar of Islamic Studies Louis Massignon, who derives it from the mystic al-Hallaj.

27 Sister Therese Lentfoehr, *Words and Silence: On the Poetry of Thomas Merton* (NY: New Directions, 1979), 50.

28 Ibid., 48.

29 Merton, *Turning Toward the World*, 230.

30 Mott, *The Seven Mountains of Thomas Merton*, 402.

31 Ibid., 138.

5.

A Grotto of Sophia Ikons

POEMS BY SUSAN MCCASLIN
GRAPHIC DESIGN BY AFTON SCHINDEL

What Is a Saint?

The pale flowers of the dogwood outside this window are
saints. The little yellow flowers that nobody notices on the
edge of that road are saints looking up into the face of God.
This leaf has its own texture and its own pattern of veins
and its own holy shape, and the bass and trout hiding in the
deep pools of the river are canonised by their beauty and
their strength. The lakes hidden among the hills are saints,
and the sea too is a saint who praises God without interrup-
tion in her majestic dance. The great, gashed, half-naked
mountain is another of God's saints.[1]
– Thomas Merton, *New Seeds of Contemplation*, 1961

For Thomas Merton, every human being, living creature, and
natural phenomenon is an embodiment of Holy Wisdom –
Sophia. His theology and his perception of the world are therefore incarnational. As William Blake puts it, "Everything that
lives is holy." Sophia is for Merton the indwelling presence of
God, ultimate Being, or Presence in the world.

As we have seen, the metaphorical and very real figure of a
mysterious young woman appears in Merton's visionary dreams
during the late 1950s. She reveals herself as "Proverb," and is

the feminine presence of what Merton experienced as God. She represents empathy, peace, and compassion at play in every living thing in the world – in bugs, birds, trees, fish, and each of us. She is the authentic self. Bugs, birds, dogs, and trees know instinctively who they are, but often we do not. Merton writes,

> For me to be a saint means to be myself. Therefore, the problem of sanctity and salvation is in fact the problem of finding out who I am and of discovering my true self...Trees and animals have no problem.[2]

The following sequence, "A Grotto of Sophia Ikons," offers poems devoted to some of Merton's personal saints from the human spheres. Readers are invited to add their own sophianic figures to this gathering, which is not meant as a comprehensive catalogue or canon. In fact, these are mostly what might be called "anti-saints" as only one, St. Thérèse of Lisieux (Merton's chosen patron saint), has been officially canonized. Yet they are holy persons, people like all of us, flawed but moving toward a kind of radical wholeness. They are human beings – imperfect, contradictory, yet radiant with joy, sorrow, human authenticity, beauty, and love that spilled over to others and to the world – and Merton cherished them. The eternal source or ground of all being, which includes and transcends all we can know or name, has for mysterious reasons chosen to speak, act, and be present in and through them. Among them are figures from the past whom Merton revered, but most were friends or correspondents during his lifetime.

Some readers may object to the word "saint" as being excessively pious. Adoration of the saints may have encouraged some to aspire to an unrealistic perfectionism. Yet Canadian singer/songwriter Leonard Cohen's statement about what constitutes a saint, from his early novel *Beautiful Losers* (1966), stands as a corrective to what is a misuse of the word.

A saint is someone who has achieved a remote human
possibility. It is impossible to say what that possibility is. I
think it has something to do with the energy of love.
Contact with this energy results in the exercise of a kind of
balance in the chaos of existence. A saint does not dissolve
the chaos; if [s/he] did the world would have changed long
ago. I do not think that a saint dissolves the chaos even for
himself [or herself], for there is something arrogant and
warlike in the notion of a [person] setting the universe in
order. It is a kind of balance that is his [her] glory.[3]

Later in the same passage Cohen refers to saints as "balancing
monsters of love." It may seem counterintuitive to apply the word
"monster" (commonly suggesting someone misshapen or mal-
formed) to a person struggling toward more integrated being.
Yet perhaps what Cohen means is that such saints can enact for
us all what is really a deeper wholeness within brokenness, and
brokenness within wholeness. They often embody a heightened
intensity that could be problematic in other contexts. Yet what
if inward grace can hone such sensitivity to unimaginably good
purposes in unfathomable ways? Then extreme perseverance, like
Dorothy Day's lifelong dedication to the poor and disenfranchised
through the Catholic Worker Movement, or the unaccountable
solidarity of Simone Weil with those suffering from war condi-
tions, present themselves as gifts.

The saint may at first glance seem idiosyncratic, like St.
Francis stripping off his clothing in the marketplace, or Merton
abandoning a potential career as a writer and English professor
to disappear into a remote Trappist monastery in the middle of
Kentucky. There is often something of the wild person in the
saint that is easy to confuse with madness, but which is poten-
tially a new revelation of love. The saint-in-progress may have
no idea why she or he is heading into the forge or for what purpose, but continues anyway. Merton expresses a state of divine

unknowing in his well-known prayer that begins, "My Lord God, I have no idea where I am going. I do not see the road ahead of me. I cannot know for certain where it will end."[4]

For me, Robert Lax brings us closest to Merton's use of the word saint. In 1938, Lax told the 23-year-old Merton that if he wanted to get on in a serious way with his spiritual aspirations, he had better pursue the business of becoming a saint.[5] At first Merton balked, but Bob's words gave him pause, then courage. At the end of his own much longer lifespan, Lax, who became a hermit-contemplative living on the Greek island of Patmos, shared this earlier insight with his young friend S.T. Georgiou: "We are meant to be holy, all of us as one. We are all called to be saints."[6]

Of course, few of us would claim to be saints, enlightened ones, or fully realized beings. To make such a claim is more likely an indication that one has *not* arrived. Yet there are people living among us, often invisibly – ordinary people often at the margins of society – for whom the designation fits. In his Fourth and Walnut epiphany, Merton noted, "[We] are all of us walking around shining like the sun."[7]

So, saints are ordinary, fragile, imperfect people, often far ahead of the rest of us on the path, but certainly not an elitist class of special ascetics or spiritually privileged ones. Saints are those who may have had direct, intimate experience of self-transcendence, powerful epiphanies, or momentary or extended revelations of divine love and wisdom. But more importantly, they have also begun to integrate such experiences into their everyday lives. They are moving forward, evolving. They feel an inner call to serve the common good and put their longings into action.

Throughout his life, Merton had a special love of orthodox icons. He collected them and carried a small one (with an image of the divine mother and child) with him on his final Asian tour. Though not Roman Catholic, I too have for many years collected icons and cultivated my own "icon corner" at home just to the left of my desk. In the course of meditating with

icons and studying the history and tradition of Eastern Orthodox icons and iconography, I have noticed striking analogues
between iconography and poem-making. I refer you to Jim Forest's *Praying with Icons* for a depth study on the making and use
of icons in Eastern Orthodox contemplative practice.[8]

Both iconographer and meditator are present to the icon
in a special way. Many who pray with icons sometimes feel
the presence of the saint indwelling the image. It is as if divine energies are actively transmitted through the icon. Therefore, a traditional icon is, for the one who reveres it, not merely
an artifact, not merely a work of art, but a mediator of ultimate reality. Likewise, the maker or reader (listener, recipi-
ent) of a sacred poem is invited to be present to the
transformative energies released in the process of the poem's
creation and ongoing life. Words, like images, are capable of
mediating or incarnating the real (an unspeakable presence
beyond and within words and images). Engaging with an icon,
then, can become an act of contemplation, a sacrament, opening through the threshold of images or words to silence and
unitive being, then leading us back again into the world.

This gathering of icon poems represents an effort to translate the spiritual practice of iconography and icon meditation
into the form of the "shape poem" through a conjoining of poetic rhythm, imagery, metaphor, symbolism, musicality, and
graphic design. Respected practitioners of the shape poem for
me include the 17th-century metaphysical poet George Herbert
among others. As in many Orthodox icons where the saint's
name is embedded somewhere within the frame, the saint's name
appears in each poem at the bottom of the graphic shape. The
icon poem, like an icon itself, requires contemplation in the
process of its making and is designed to evoke a contemplative
state in the reader/viewer. As the traditional icon painter prays
throughout the process of creating the icon and blesses it before giving it to another, so I attempted to surrender my full

attention to the words and images as they emerged and were crafted, then sent each poem out with a blessing. Perhaps the Eastern analogy to the icon is the mandala, where meditation on an image of wholeness invites mental-emotional-spiritual participation, which may awaken a corresponding wholeness in the participant.

Thanks are due to my niece Afton Schindel, an accomplished graphic designer and collaborator in this creative process. Each icon, like each saint, is unique. Afton and I worked together to ensure as much as possible that, in the words of poet Denise Levertov, form "is never more than a revelation of content."[9] In other words, we did not simply pour the words of my poem into a chosen iconic shape, but sought the form, font, and line breaks that revealed themselves as most integral to the words and essence of the saint.

For many, Merton reclaims and expands the notion of saint-hood to help us actualize the energies of these seemingly exceptional souls as accessible to all. We are all saints, anti-saints, and saints-in-progress in our clustered and individual sheen, always stepping slowly or quickly into the oneness that has never abandoned us. I'd like to close this preface with a poem I wrote when immersed in the creation of these poems, since it expresses my sense of Merton as saint and as a gatherer of saints in his garden of love.

A Finger Pointing to the Moon

[Merton] will not let me look at him for long:
he will, finally, persuade me to look in the direction he is looking.
– Rowan Williams, *A Silent Action: Engagements with Thomas Merton*

Merton built a personality
so he could disappear

was and was not
his layered, shifting self

that time-shelf, reef —
yet not less

than his many voices
and words

not artless
but art, less ego —

another art-full
encomium

praise-singer
singing

1   Thomas Merton, *New Seeds of Contemplation* (NY: New Directions, 1961), 30-31.
2   Ibid., 31.
3   Leonard Cohen, *Stranger Music* (Toronto: McClelland & Stewart, 1993), 126.
    This passage first appeared in Leonard Cohen's novel *Beautiful Losers*
    (McClelland & Stewart, 1966).
4   Thomas Merton, *Thoughts in Solitude* (NY: Farrar, Straus & Giroux, 1999), 79.
5   Thomas Merton, *The Seven Storey Mountain* (NY: Harcourt, Brace & Co., 1948),
    238.
6   S.T. Georgiou, *The Way of the Dreamcatcher: Spirit Lessons with Robert Lax: Poet,
    Peacemaker, Sage* (Ottawa, Ontario: Novalis, 2002), 63.
7   Thomas Merton, *Conjectures of a Guilty Bystander* (NY: Doubleday, 1968), 157.
8   Jim Forest, *Praying with Icons* (Maryknoll, New York: Orbis Books, 1997),. Note:
    Jim Forest, a friend and correspondent of Merton's, was one of the Milwaukee
    14 who burned their draft cards in protest against the Vietnam War. Jim
    underwent imprisonment for civil disobedience and was supported by both
    Dorothy Day and Thomas Merton for his non-violent activism.
9   Denise Levertov, "Some Notes on Organic Form," in *The Poet in the World* (New
    York: New Directions, 1973), 13.

In the hospital, when
six-year-old Tom's
mother lay dying, she wouldn't
let him see her pain.
He later wrote she had been
cold, distanced, demanding,
not adding intelligent, loving, sensitive.
In *Tom's Book* she recorded his every infant
word and step, leaving a legacy of journal-keeping:
"When he hears music he begins to dance, changing
to fast or slow steps as the music changes. Sometimes
when he is playing he sings. When we go out, he seems
conscious of everything. Sometimes he puts up
his arms and cries out, "O Sun! O Joli!"
She, his broken poetry wing,
his absent-present Sophia
St. Ruth Jenkins Merton

Tom's best friend at Columbia.
They became riffing jesters,
Sephardic clowns, cartoonists.
Bob the elongated and fluid,
Tom the muscular and compact,
linked by jiving jazz talk.
So many ways to sign off
in their cache of anti-letters,
Tom as Demosthenes, Bob as Sam.
Chums of the thousand names.
If Tom hadn't disappeared
to the other side of the Asian mountain,
he might have landed on Patmos' rocky shore,
Bob's home, place of minimalist largesse,
rested his head on the stone pillow
carved by the seer who dreamed in the cave
where "we are all called to be saints,"
as said St. Robert Lax

While
at Columbia University
(1 9 3 8)
Tom picks up Lax's shy Hindu friend
at Grand Central Station,
little monk of the yellow turban,
white robe, and sneakers (Keds),
who, though baffled
at the west's wealth and waste,
later urges: "Read the mystical books
written by Christians (Augustine, à Kempis)."
Delve, delve. So he who became Thomas Merton,
(bestselling Catholic convert),
comes to the universals of the Christian
contemplative way through a humble
guru from the east,
St. Mahanambrata
Brahmachari

The
patriarchy required
its woman small, sugary, sexless,
so you complied, refused even to lean back
in your chair, ate little, performed the thousand self-
mortifications, but at the end delivered your Little Way, way
of a small white stone; then after your death
white petals rained from the sky
past the heads of bishops, priests,
prioresses, abbots, popes,
your voice boomed,
b l o o m e d
St. Thérèse de
Lisieux

In
another life, Dorothy,
long-limbed blonde Athena
of the chiselled cheekbones,
could have been a fashion model
or an Amazon warrior. Yet hers,
peaceful resistance like that of Gandhi and King.
First the early atheism, the abortion,
the single parenting, the abandonment by lovers,
one who found her "too radical, the other "too religious."
So when she turned to see Christ in the skilled,
unemployed worker, the homeless, the destitute,
she made her heart "a Christ room," hospitality chamber,
endlessly open. Still a utopian pragmatist,
she is standing in the bread lines,
picketing at nuclear weapons sites, suffering house arrest
indicting corporate capitalism, decrying global warming
through all our cold, hot wars. "Don't call me a saint," she said,
"I don't want to be dismissed that easily."
Then added: "We are all called to be saints."
Whenever we love the enemy who could be ourselves,
we bear the ageless braided beauty
of the universal worker
St. Dorothy Day

You
for whom
the kingdom of heaven is
insect bird reptile lily, in whom
the kingdom rises, evolving, revolving
toward origin into mystery, new
Nicaraguas, where all beings rise
religion-free, breathing, out, in,
just like God the Breath in
St. Ernesto
Cardenal

In '61, Tom hovered at your door, calling you
one of his "best friends."
Through the Black Death, famine,
continental wars, you, English anchoress,
enclosed in your chosen anchor-hold
just to the side of the church,
had so much to be pessimistic about,
you, the unlikeliest person to assert,
"All shall be well." Yet here we are holed up
in our dark; drones flying, fear fuelling
our terrible love of war, capitalism seizuring,
oceans acidifying, the beautiful creatures
dying, as we move steadily toward our greed-made
hells, or (what seems less likely) the birth
of our empathetic beast.
Such a small peephole of hope
out of which to gaze.
Yet gaze you did, held in the paradox
of hope and despair. Out of the wounded heart
you still chant, "All shall be well,
and all shall be well."
After gazing on human perversity,
the mercy touched you deep,
hauling your shrewd theological mind
to joy and praise, you who,
as long as you stared into God,
"could find no wrath," holding
in the hand that held yours
the tiny hazelnut of our being,
you, wise-hearted
St. Julian of Norwich

The sisters of Loretto,
who lived near Gethsemani,
weren't being heard by the cardinals, bishops, & priests,
so Merton proposed a few anti-workshops
just before he died, where together they lounged on the lawn
by the ponds. He showed them his hermitage,
his bongos, leveled with them about male privilege,
concurred with Mary Daly about the death of God the Father,
studied Betty Friedan's *The Feminine Mystique*,
how women (especially nuns) were socialized to be mysterious,
passive—other. "Be fully human" he urged,
"Don't ask permission, just act."
"No more lining up with the structures."
So Mary Luke went on to make policy
at Vatican II, travelled to Saigon,
urged women's ordination,
Buddhist-Christian dialogue,
protested at nuclear weapons sites,
this small, puissant
St. Mary Luke Tobin

With
long   black   hair   gleaming,
you step into the hermitage
Of the famous monk, robust
in mid-life, looking like a cross
between Henry Miller and Pablo Picasso,
you on the parabola of youth,
he in the tumult of his midsummer love,
playing   over   and   over   your   ballad
"Silver   Dagger,"   lament   for   a   mother
who,   betrayed   by   her   husband,   teaches
her   daughter   to   sleep   alone
with   a   dagger   at   her   side.   Did   he   find   there
traces   of   what   seemed   his   betrayal
of   M.   and   of   himself?
When   you   keen   against   the   murder   of   Joe   Hill,
union   activist,   newly   disempowered   workers
rise   before   our   eyes   and   we   long   for   a   time
when   songs   could   change   the   world.
Your   voice   still   as   strong   as   in   those   heady   days,
only deeper, fiercer
like the luminous beauty
of St.   Joan Baez

You
shaped   my
young mythopoetic
i m a g i n a t i o n ,
then argued a poetics of political
e n g a g e m e n t .
When crossing the border to Canada (1969),
I   absorbed   your   anti-war   hymns
for   napalm-smeared   Vietnamese   children.
Years   later,   in   Tom's   posthumous   journals,
I learned how (a year before his death)
you   spent an afternoon with him
and Wendell Berry at the   hermitage.
You, daughter of a Hasidic, Russian, Jewish father
and mystic Welsh mother, stepped
once again into the mystic stream.
When   composing
"On the Feast for St. Thomas Didymas,"
you plunged from doubt to faith,
at last settling near Mount Rainier,
staring up with eyes wide open
from the great rainforest floor
where a waterfall poured down
"mercy within mercy within mercy,"
t i l l   y o u   b e c a m e
what   you   had   always   been,
St. Denise Levertov

"Few
writers have a better
understanding
of our calamities," Merton wrote of Weil.
Their paths never crossed,
though in '42 she took mass
at Corpus Christi in New York
where he had knelt the year before.
"Absolutely unmixed attention
is prayer," said Simone, and from her saying
deer slipped from the woods behind Tom's hermitage,
multiplying in his eye like first art from the dark,
secret caves of Lascaux. He loved her for her
"effective nonviolence," not pacifism but peaceful resistance.
When she parsed her indivisible attention to workers,
grape-gatherers & soldiers, her empathy woke
new solidarities. When she recited
George Herbert's "Love (III)," the Jewish
and universal Jesus claimed her,
setting her down just outside
the institutions on that liminal
ground she called Metaxu,
place of separation and linkage
into which all blessings flow,
as they did from her
in whom affliction
showed its gravity as grace,
St. Simone
W e i l

You
met face to
face just once,
Gethsemani, May 26, 1966.
Tom in the middle of his amputation from M.
"Nhất Hạnh Is My Brother," he wrote.
Monks, poets, activists, opposed to the Vietnam War,
conjoined mindfulness and contemplation,
one long intake of a common breath.
Your friend, boundary-breaker, poet, Zen master,
toiled in the war fields for the damaged.
"I must speak out for peace," he declared.
At a retreat in Vancouver, 2011,
I entered his poetics of brevity:
"I bring my mind back to my body,
so that I may be here for you."
"No mud, no lotus."
"Be beautiful, be yourself."
"Peace is every step."
I knew then what Tom had written:
"Just the way he opens the door and enters a room
demonstrates his understanding. He is a true monk."
Now Merton is beyond, Thầy here,
yet both lightly touch in the Pure Land,
the Kingdom of Heaven,
studying together at the University of Compassion,
living Buddhas, living Christs.
"The bread we eat is the whole cosmos," said
St. Thích Nhất Hạnh

High
in the Himalayas,
such an attunement—East and West.
"I have seldom met anyone with whom
I clicked so well," wrote Merton.
His Holiness needed to know
if the Western monks had a method for
moving through the mystical stages.
They agreed that withdrawing from the world
isn't an end, but the base for engagement.
Tenzin told how even when he and his people
fled Tibet, he didn't see the Chinese as enemies.
Outside his Dharamsala residence people continued
strewing lotus flowers and prayers.
His Holiness, 33, Merton, 53, only a month from
his Bangkok death. After their three conversations,
he named Tom a "Catholic Geshe," fellow monk,
then 28 years later, came to Gethsemani to
drape a white prayer shawl and
mindfulness meditations over
his friend's grave, he the oceanic
St. Tenzin Gyatso, the 14th
Dalai Lama

In the brokenness
you are the arrow of my human eros
shot at the heart of the mystery
a burnt man aflame
saintly like all
fragments of the hidden
wholeness
you never left
but leaving made more whole
St. Thomas Merton

Saint Alpha
St. Songster singing
St. Everywoman piecemeal
St. Everyman unemployed
St. Somebody exploited
St. Alphabet broken
St. Somebody Nobody
St. Not Knowing who we are
St. Jack of Diamonds shining
St. Broken-Open overhauled
St. Failure in rehab
St. Poverty the Christ
St. Hale and Shattered Shard
St. Long-Lingering Light
St. Omega

6.

Love and Solitude

A Cache of Love Letters
for Tom and Margie

SUSAN MCCASLIN

Love and solitude are the one ground of true maturity and
freedom. Solitude that is just solitude and nothing else (i.e.
excludes everything else but solitude) is worthless. True
solitude embraces everything, for it is the fullness of love
that rejects nothing and no one, is open to All in All.
— Merton's journal, April 14, 1966

Love is our true destiny. We do not find the meaning of life
by ourselves alone — we find it with another. We do not
discover the secret of our lives merely by study and calculation in our isolated meditations. The meaning of our life is a
secret that has to be revealed to us in love, by the one we
love.
— Thomas Merton, from "Love and Need: Is Love a Package
or a Message?"

Dear Tom & Margie,
   When I recently reread Tom's journals written after you
two fell in love at the hospital in Louisville in the spring of 1966
(I was 19 at the time), I remembered my fascination with the
television mini-series from the 1980s based on the novel *The*

Thorn Birds. The series starred Richard Chamberlain as a sexy priest who fell madly in love with Meggie, a younger Australian woman. Was your love merely an episodic escapade based on some "monk mystique?" A "thorny" issue indeed. For me, you two aren't a tawdry soap opera drama. There's something more. Some longing for wholeness.

Turns out, through a magical union of luck, work, and love, I married a nine-years-younger man and we've celebrated our 40th anniversary.

You two didn't get a chance to step out of the forge into the fires of the everyday.

S

Dear Margie,

When I was 24 I fell desperately in love with my thesis advisor at graduate school, a man about my father's age. He was, for me, Socrates or William Blake. A charismatic poet-scholar, debonair, witty, intelligent, kind – and gay. Had he asked, I would have run away with him to a Greek island, where we would have written poems and shared Platonic love. Perhaps I even thought I might convert him to heterosexual love, though I told myself it was his mind I cared for. Such naiveté! Yet I loved him absolutely at the time. Fortunately, my advisor remained in his professional role, guiding me deftly through my thesis. If he noticed I was smitten, he didn't once show it.

Now I'm cabling these somewhat impertinent, un-dialogic field letters to you two silent, invisible recipients because I still wonder about the existential absurdity of your affair with its wild improbabilities and rich contradictions.

As the mother of a daughter not far from the age you were when you met Tom, I have to consider the significant age gap, how raw we all are at 24, our brains not quite fully formed. If my daughter had developed a relationship with a man old enough to be her father when she was Margie's age, I think (had she asked) I would have advised her to reconsider. These days society is more aware of the ethics involved in not only the age gap but the power gap between the two of you. Yet he was a vibrant 51, an age that seems young to me now. I marvel at your youthful authenticity and lament your lack of voice in the aftermath.

With you two, I enter again the league of impossible lovers: Tristan and Isolde, Romeo and Juliet. In your case, a slightly older Juliet with a middle-aged Romeo. Adam and Eve not yet quarrelling and exiled, but not sailing along smoothly either.

Yet as Tom said, "Thank God for this blessed disturbance."[1] A day later, he wrote a love poem, "Louisville Airport."

> Here on the foolish grass...
> [W]e with the gentle liturgy
> of shy children have permitted God
> to make again that first world...[2]

So how could he, after finding it, leave that Eden?

S

Dear Margie,

By all Tom's accounts, you didn't have reservations about abandoning yourself fully to his love. One gets the sense that you loved unreservedly and would have unquestionably married this bestselling author and spiritual mentor, had he agreed.

Rumour has it you were willing to break things off with your fiancé. Tom suggests in places in his journals that you were the one who loved more, but who can say?

Yet unlike the famous monk, had you married him, you wouldn't have had to rethink decades of dedication to a path of contemplation.

How do you see things now? You are still alive, but silent; he is alive in the here-now of his words.

His poems and letters are all we have of you, along with the sometimes-invasive ruminations of scholars. I admire you for not writing a memoir titled *My Affair with Thomas Merton*. No doubt a bestseller, a real page turner!

S

Dear Tom,

Years before you met, one could say you dreamed of M. in myriad forms. A parapsychologist might call these precognitions.

> I am embraced with determined and virginal passion by a young Jewish girl. She clings to me and will not let go, and I get to like the idea...I ask her name and she says her name is Proverb.[3]

In the late 1950s you were reading the Russian mystical theologians. In 1960, after being hospitalized for several days, you wrote about waking to the voice of a nurse. In 1961, you composed your long liturgical poem "Hagia Sophia," where Wisdom is Nurse, Mother, Sister, Beloved, the female Christ, the *Ousia* or very Being of Being, gently waking the sleeper and setting his feet on the road.

Archetype and reality converged.

> [T]he archetypal M. and the reality merge together: the M. I love in the depths of my heart is not symbolic and not just the everyday M. either, but the deep, mysterious, personal, unique potential that is in her...[4]

No more running, Tom. The divine and the human aligned. The archetypal and the temporal. Nurse as healer.

A new vow of obedience arose in you as a poem, "I Always Obey My Nurse."

Because I am always broken
I obey my nurse
who in her grey eyes and her mortal breast
Holds an immortal love the wise have fractured.
Because we have both been broken we can tell
that God did not make death.[5]

S

Dear Margie,

Even in the autumn of 1966, when he'd made up his mind it was over, he linked you to Proverb-Sophia when passing through your home city.

And I walked through Cincinnati station with the words of
Proverbs 8 in my mind: "And my delights were to be with
the children of men!"– I have never forgotten this, it struck
me so forcefully then! Strange connections in my deepest
heart– between M. and the "Wisdom" figure– and Mary–
the Feminine in the Bible– Eve etc.– Paradise– Wisdom."[6]

Eight years earlier, on February 28, 1958, Holy Wisdom met him in a visionary dream in the figure of a young Jewish girl. In his journal he called her Proverb. Shortly afterward, on March 19, 1958, Wisdom in her incarnate form embraced him through an epiphany at the corner of Forth and Walnut in downtown Louisville when she shone forth in the faces of ordinary women, ordinary people on the street. This moment stands as the break-through where he affirms his essential unity with humanity and moves away from his notion of himself as cloistered, apart. "As if waking from a dream– the dream of my separateness, of the 'special' vocation to be different."[7]

All these presentiments gathered for an expanded moment in your face. I can't help but see these appearances of Sophia as a progressive revelation leading to a deepening of his commitment to intimacy, and indeed unity, with his fellow human beings.

Is it a burden or an honour to carry such a weight? Or are we all archetypal and human when truly seen?

S

Dear Tom,

Rereading your frenetic outpourings, I don't doubt your love for M. Yet I can't help but see that your life was a series of contradictions, and you found yourself, "travelling in the belly of a paradox."[8] It was given you to hold the tensions, and you did. Flawed human like us all, a work in progress.

You take the journal to the level of art form; art as process, not product. You see the multiple sides of everything through your own multiple masks, somehow all of them moving toward some crazy, cracked wholeness.

Reading your entries is like staring at the backside of a tapestry displaying random, tangled threads. Is there some kind of pattern apparent from the front?

Even your most ardent feelings about M. aren't absolute. You speak of how at last you know you can love "with an awful completeness."[9] Then six months later you renounce the affair as "very silly."[10] Occasionally you describe it as an awakening to which you couldn't quite rise. Listen to you lecturing yourself.

> You had your last chance to get with reality. You found what few people manage to find, someone made for you, for whom you were made. You should have had the courage to throw everything overboard and simply go and live with her. You should have gambled on love, and you would have won. As it is, you are stuck with a futile and absurd existence in which besides *knowing* your failure and your ambiguities, you will now spend the rest of your life manufacturing alibis."[11]

You are your own most stringent jury and judge.

Your turmoil makes you dear. I can't trust all those clashing voices and masks, but neither can you. One mask may repudiate another, but the poems and journals don't repudiate themselves, stretched present-wise across the length of M.'s silences.

You name your jazzed-up, remembered behaviours "the ex-priest alcoholic driven to drink by M.," the "wild faun bit."[12] They become a fascinating dance I watch and retreat from and embrace. Acceptance-repudiation, intimacy-withdrawal, second-guessing, back-and-forth, self-recriminations, guilt-weeping.

Because of your utter honesty, we become you. Rationalizing, self-blaming, forgiving, you open up the entire messy process we all live each day when you say,

> What I see is this: that while I imagine I was functioning fairly successfully, I was living a sort of patched up, crazy existence, a series of rather hopeless improvisations, a life of unreality in many ways...There is "I"– this patchwork, this bundle of questions and doubts and obsessions, this gravitation to silence and to the woods and to love. This incoherence!![13]

Here's to blessed incoherence.

You are us.

Me.

S

Dear Margie,

More and more there is simply no urge in me to judge. No place for judgment.

Still, I wonder whether there was a place in you for anger. Did you ask yourself if he loved the idea of falling in love more than the act of loving? Did you think him selfish, fearful of commitment, living mostly in his head? Did you feel betrayed?

Perhaps he got past self-judgment. He was honest about the process, constantly shifting back and forth about whether his time with you was an immature episode or a profound, eternal love he couldn't make whole. Lapse, fling, or transformation? Maybe all three.

Is that point of suffering where you found yourselves pinned also the *point vierge* into which he finally disappeared? Yours was a crucifixion of romantic love.

What went through your mind when you first heard the news of his death?

Again, not mine to ask.

S

Dear Margie,

In a June 19, 1966 entry, after reading Camus' *Sisyphus*, Tom stumbles upon what he calls "these touching lines" by a poet published in the *New Yorker*.

Everyone has left me
except my muse
that good nurse.
She stays in my hand
Like a wild white mouse.[14]

He goes on in the same entry to associate the mouse in the poem with you, Margie, and switches to address you directly: "Dear, never leave me. Have you perhaps found out the art of being that mouse in the hermitage after all? You have been so close all morning, so quiet, so sweet, so gentle and so patient. How could I ever be without you?"

Then, on May 6, 1967, Tom notes in his journal that after finishing Camus' *The Plague*, he finds a dead mouse on his doorstep, "a white-footed mouse."

Is the mouse you, Margie? Are his notes tokens of his guilt?

Is he lamenting how he "murdered" his love? Or expressing guilt for killing some potential between the two of you, that small, fragile creature of purity and wholeness who has quietly crept into the sanctuary of his hermitage?

Is he the female mouse at the door? Did he feel he had killed his own feminine self, or destroyed his potential to love and be loved?

A further layer: I later discovered that earlier in 1963, before he even met you, Tom wrote in his journal of discovering a titmouse (a small bird) that died due to the monastery's use of pesticides.[15] Could the image of the dead mouse tie not only to the loss of your shared intimacy, but extend back to his awakening ecological consciousness?

You, Gaia, Sophia, Tom's feminine self, our expanded Selves in intimate union with nature and with one other – one continuing lineage.

S

Dear Tom,

On the way to Asia on your last journey, when the comparative religion scholar Huston Smith asked you about the difficulties of keeping a monk's vows of poverty, chastity, and obedience, you quipped, "Poverty is a snap. Chastity is more difficult but manageable. But obedience – obedience is a bugger!"[16]

Given that you had just emerged from your struggle over whether to make a life with M., your response isn't surprising. Given your long struggle with your often controlling and intractable Abbot Dom James Fox, and your position as a maverick within the religious structures, obedience surely must have been the hardest thing.

Yet I wonder if you ever saw your entanglement with M. as a test. I think of the young seeker Siddhartha leaving his wife and child, or St. Anthony in the desert fighting off temptation.

Perhaps celibacy wasn't a matter of dogma or church authority for you. Perhaps it was not simply a rejection of the body and the feminine, or even tied to a sense of sin. Perhaps it was part of a covenant with God you made as a young man, and being single, *monokos*, a solitary, became the seed of your deepening life of contemplation and central to your legacy.

The question of sexual abstinence as an element in the spiritual path is present in many spiritual traditions. When all that sexual energy isn't released through bodily expression, does it rise up the spine as kundalini fire? Even in ancient Taoism there are teachings about how reproductive energy, life-force energy, and spiritual energy are various manifestations of one higher power circulating and flowing through all. Spiritual practices in both East and West have been tied to the sublimation or transformation of these energies. Celibacy has been seen in monastic traditions as one route to enlightenment or cosmic consciousness.

Yet as more recent exposures of systemic sexual abuse within the Roman Catholic Church and other religious institutions have made apparent, institutionally required celibacy can be tied to perverse forms of sexual expression and victimization of the powerless. It is clear you struggled with the call to life-long celibacy. These issues of sexual abuse came to the fore after your time, but you were fully cognizant of various forms of corruption within institutional structures.

Real chastity. What is it? For me it has less to do with sexual abstinence than with purity of heart.

Your vows of poverty, chastity, and obedience (not just as rules, but as ways of living) were profoundly important to you. You kept returning to them. They weren't sacred to you just because of the Church; they were integral to your identity as a contemplative – your spiritual vocation.

There are times though, when I see you rationalizing your decision to leave Margie in order to avoid becoming a contemplative within the quotidian reality of marriage. Perhaps you couldn't see yourself living a conventional married life, divvying up household chores or raising kids. A '60s lifestyle in the burbs must have seemed inseparable from materialism, getting and spending, television and potato chips. Perhaps you feared you would lose your solitude and the freedom to study, read, and write that you had fought for in your long struggle to become a hermit at Gethsemani.

My husband and I, in another era not far behind yours, sometimes think we have managed to become, each in our way, both solitary and communal, chaste and sexual. Aspiring contemplatives in another mode.

S

Dear Margie,

What's your take on the contemplative life versus conventional marriage? Did you think, when he started to distance himself from you, that Tom was trapped in his sense that marriage would likely prove antithetical to his spiritual life? Or are you now glad he didn't marry you? After all, we now know you later married and had a family. Did hurt or even anger linger?

A journal entry from May 9, 1966 shows he did briefly consider the possibility of marriage.

> It is, however, now, to me a really serious option: that if in the near future the way *does* open for a married clergy, I should take it.[17]

There were no strong models for a contemplative life within marriage in the structures you both knew. Some monastics broke free from their institutions and made lives with their lovers.

I remember taking my husband to hear poet William Everson read in Vancouver. It was near the end of Everson's life when he was struggling with Parkinson's disease. Everson, like Tom, had undergone a dramatic conversion, becoming Brother Antoninus, "the Beat Friar," but ended up breaking his vows with the Dominicans and marrying his lover. His prose poem *River-Root: A Syzygy* is a racy read, a radical paean to sexuality worthy of William Blake. Like Tom, he was a pacifist and involved with the Catholic Worker Movement. He left his order in 1969, the year after Tom died, to marry a woman many years his junior. The parallels are striking but the differences more so.

Tom loved Rilke, who said, "Love consists in this, that two solitudes protect and touch and greet each other."[18] I like to dream of "two integrities" as a union of apparently irreconcilable opposites. While I don't think Rilke sustained this state in his personal life, he could imagine it. I dream of "two integrities," complementary polarities both distinct and one.

Singer-poet Leonard Cohen writes about the loss we feel when we seem to fail love.

> Everybody knows that the naked man and woman
> Are just a shining artefact of the past.[19]

Though you and Tom might have plunged into another kind of wholeness, there was no time. He would be dead within two years.

In the end he just couldn't shift and turn.

I hope your life became another wholeness. I hope that for you there is nothing to answer, or resolve, or regret.

S

Dear Margie,

Tom's journals say you challenged him during a phone conversation on something he said about "detachment." Possibly he had in mind his developing sense of Buddhist "non-attachment."

Brava! You wouldn't let him get away with fear and self-protectiveness masquerading as spirituality. He was quick to point out that non-attachment to outcomes isn't the same thing as emotional detachment.

> But of course to talk about detachment when you are in love is just nonsense... I am in much deeper than I ever was before... (In the light of M.'s love I realized for the first time how deeply I was loved back in those days by girls whose names I have even forgotten.)[20]

And this:

> It is not simply a passion, a bodily need (though the physical reactions are profound!); it is a deep love of our heart. I feel I must fully surrender to it because it will change and heal my life in a way that I fear, but I think it is necessary – in a way that will force me first of all to receive an enormous amount of love (which to tell the truth I have often feared).[21]

So much fear, so many barricades. There is no dismissing this relationship as "all about sex," though the body has its claims.
Yet he left you more:

> Poor darling, I can see how rough this is on her – in some ways worse than it is for me. And in some ways not as bad. But one thing is sure: where love is serious, there is real suffering.[22]

S

Dear Tom & Margie,
For me your story is a Celtic love knot inscribed in the trunk of a tree. Precisely, the beloved tree outside my kitchen win-

dow, a Douglas fir I named Victorine.

It's delightful you shared not only laughter over Peanuts cartoons in the Louisville hospital, not only each other's bodies, but poems. Poems as bodies; bodies as poems.

Of your midsummer trysts Tom says, "We talked and loved and scarcely ate anything, but drank Chianti and read poems and loved and loved." Poetry was ever the central course in your picnics and rendezvous. Feasts of love, food, words. "Paradise Feasts,"[23] Tom called them, and afterwards wrote poem after poem in what he called "a Bob Dylan style."

Even the names of your meeting days and places are resonant: Derby Day, Annunciation Day, Cherokee Park. Tom cherished the places where you loved, revisiting them alone like Stations of the Cross after things went awry. He wrote love poems, 18 or more, that still illuminate your affair, making of it not fiasco but liturgy.

How you two poem together.

Letter-writing is lovemaking is poetry.

Is the universe constantly writing us all love-letters that we seldom receive?

Tom, you claimed your love drew forth poems that are among your best, and I concur.

One you inscribed in your journal is from M. herself. I see it now as a "found poem" that I return to you both as "M.'s Song."

The happiest I have ever been
is when I took care of you in the hospital.
Being without you isn't the hardest thing –
It's not being able to give you anything
except thoughts and prayers.

You keep me, you guard me,
you protect me in all my ways.

We have been given each other to love,
to love totally without having
to hold back a thing, with complete abandon.

There are no fears,
no pretenses, just knowing
that somewhere you exist
and are loving me as I love you
sustains me...[24]

Take this raft of belated love letters for two lovers, both of whom were younger then than I am today.

S

Dear Margie,

I'm thinking of Tom's mother, Ruth, who recorded his infancy and childhood in conscientious detail in what she called "Tom's Book." Surely, she transmitted the habit of journal-keeping to her son. I don't think you were a mother figure to him; yet I intuit something of her playfulness in you.

Not being allowed to say farewell to his mother when she lay dying in the hospital must have been traumatic. Did he begin then to distance himself from intimacy with women out of fear of repeating the shock of that loss? His apparently shallow and exploitative relations with women at Cambridge before his conversion seem part of a flight and a distancing.

I'm no psychologist, but I wonder if, despite the potential damage to you both, his relationship with you helped him repair the superficial relationships of his profligate youth. Rumour has it he impregnated a young woman while at Cambridge. Perhaps you and Tom were about the same emotional age. Am I absolving Tom too much?

As early as 1959 Tom was reading Paul Evdokimov's *Woman and the Salvation of the World* in which the restoration of the divine image in humanity is presented as both male and female.[25] Then in 1965, not that long before he met you, he was poring through Karl Stern's *The Flight from Woman*, an analysis of our culture's fear of the feminine that likely raised spectres from Tom's own life.[26]

After your relationship with Tom ended, he confessed to Rosemary Ruether that he had been defensive with her because he was afraid of strong women like his mother. If true, then as nurse and sophianic muse, you were in some sense a healer.

In January of 1968, about a year before he died, Merton was reading Iranian psychologist Reza Arasteh's *Final Integration in the Adult Personality* about a transcultural consciousness where male-female principles are unified in each individual.[27] In his own essay "Final Integration: Toward a Monastic Therapy," a response to Arasteh, Merton writes of feminine wisdom as the unifying principle, citing an ancient liturgical prayer to the Theotokos, or divine mother, as Holy Wisdom.

> *Through your love, bind my soul.* Make me unified, that from the mass of my many states of soul, a single soul, *anima*, may arise. Through her religious structure, woman represents this act of life-giving integration, the only one that is able to stop the enterprise of demolition and dehumanization which entraps the modern masculine spirit...[28]

I think that intimacy with you, Margie, helped him find this balance within himself and in the world. It helped him become more fully a transcultural person who could embrace not only the feminine but the other, in all kinds of people.

And if you were for him, even briefly, the humanity of the Theotokos, the God-bearer Sophia, then what was he for you?

S

Dear Tom,

In the journals, you relate how on August 20, 1968 you burned M.'s letters in the pines, calling your love for M. "an incredible stupidity."[29]

How could you repudiate your love in such a dramatic way? Why not just let it be? Was this your attempt to assert closure?

Or was this just another dramatic gesture, no more final than the others?

It didn't work Tom, for you wrote after the break up,

> The discovery that in each other we find the meaning of life and the universe – that we are capable together of being a microcosm, a whole world, a summary of it all. And then to have the history of this world cut short – we spin in space like empty capsules. And yet no. There is a certain fullness in my life now, even without her. Something that was never there before.[30]

The conflagration was another station, not the entire way.

S

Dear Tom,

For what it's worth – here's how I see things now.

You were moving steadily toward embracing the feminine in yourself and in living women in the last few years of your life. You sought integration but knew you couldn't achieve it through your ego. Being with M. – irresponsible, immature, and episodic as the encounter might seem from outside – became part of your growth. You left for Asia at least knowing you could fully love and be loved by another.

> I feel that somehow my sexuality has been made real and decent again after years of rather frantic suppression (for though I thought I had it all truly controlled, this was an

illusion). I feel less sick, I feel human, I am grateful for her
love which is so totally mine. All the beauty of it comes from
this that we are *not* just playing, we belong totally to each
other's love (except for the vow that prevents the last
complete surrender).[31]

Whether there was an equivalent gift for Margie we cannot
know. You said you wanted her to move on and find fulfillment,
to live her own life. The above reference to how your "vow"
prevented "the last complete surrender" argues you two held
off on consummating your relationship. However, Paul Elie, in
his study, *The Life You Save May Be Your Own: An American Pilgrimage*, draws from unpublished journal entries that confirm
the relationship was sexually consummated.[32]

So having experienced union with a woman (whether physically "consummated" or not), you went forward to your death
in Asia, past the dark duels with ego. At the feet of the stone
Buddhas you were "jerked clean" from the succession of temporal selves that were and were not you. It is my hope you
achieved blessedness like that of which Yeats wrote in "A Dialogue of Self and Soul."

When such as I cast out remorse
So great a sweetness flows into the breast
We must laugh and we must sing,
We are blest by everything,
Everything we look upon is blest.[33]

S

Dear Tom & Margie,
     A short missive. Quoting Tom again from an entry on Sep-
tember 6, 1966.
     Too much analyzing.[34]

182

I hurl this instructive missive at myself.

S

Dear Tom,

There's a dream of yours I can't forget, a dream of M. swimming just off shore, beckoning you to join her, but you cannot. She is naked and wants you to come into the shining waters. One of the monks is in the way. She looks "disconsolate and alone," but you can't reach her.[35]

Paradise weeps in you.[36]

S

Dear Tom & Margie,

Do you still carry each other inside? She, you? You, her? Do memory and desire linger beyond death? I last saw you, Tom, in a dream.

You were holding forth to a small group of students seated on a lawn in a kind of cosmic collegiate system, a heavenly university. The building behind you didn't resemble a typical religious institution but was made of blocks of some type of clear Plexiglas that let in the light. The rooms inside the building were as full of plants and trees as the forested grounds. You were a peripatetic philosopher in jeans, no sign of a habit or cowl. Wildly excited, your clear blue eyes danced. You were still speaking, writing poetry, still in love with the natural world. You leaned against a pine for a moment.

Now you two are both absent presences, present absences, wreathed in mystery. Tom has disappeared into the mystery beyond death. Margie is alive in this world but wrapped in the mystery of silence.

Here in this understudy of entangled, entangling love letters, an energy field rises where I step lively inside your living flames of love, burnt yet unscathed, changed in the heat of imaginal conversations. My love letters to you, mere footnotes, publicly private, privately public, float across a computer screen to linger in a book.

May our words not be merely about you two or about me, but about where our lives and letters point.

S

1   Thomas Merton, journal entry May 6, 1966, *Learning to Love: The Journals of Thomas Merton*, Vol.6: 1966-1967, ed. Christine Bochan (NY: HarperCollins, 1997), 51.

2   Merton, journal entry May 7, 1966, *Learning to Love*, 52.

3   Thomas Merton, journal entry Feb. 28, 1958, *A Search for Solitude: The Journals of Thomas Merton*, Vol.3: 1952-1960, ed. Lawrence S. Cunningham (San Francisco: HarperCollins, 1996), 176.

4   Merton, journal entry June 22, 1966, *Learning to Love*, 328.

5   Merton, journal entry May 9, 1966, *Learning to Love*, 56.

6   Merton, journal entry Sept. 6, 1966, *Learning to Love*, 130-131.

7   Merton, *A Search for Solitude*, 182.

8   Thomas Merton, opening epigraph in *The Sign of Jonas* (NY: Harcourt Brace & Co., 1981).

9   Merton, journal entry May 9, 1966, *Learning to Love*, 54.

10 Merton, journal entry Nov. 1, 1966, *Learning to Love*, 155.

11 Merton, journal entry June 23, 1966, *Learning to Love*, 337.

12 Merton, journal entry June 24, 1966, *Learning to Love*, 344.

13 Merton, journal entry Sept. 5, 1966, *Learning to Love*, 125.

14 Merton, journal entry June 19, 1966, *Learning to Love*, 318.

15 Merton, journal entry April 1963, *Turning Toward the World: The Journals of Thomas Merton*, Vol. 4: 1960-1963, ed. Victor A. Kramer (NY: HarperSanFrancisco, 1996), 312.

16 Huston Smith, *And Live Rejoicing: Chapters from a Charmed Life* (Novato, California: New World Library, 2012), 181.

17 Merton, journal entry May 9, 1966, *Learning to Love*, 55.

18 Rainer Maria Rilke, *Letters to a Young Poet*, trans. Stephen Mitchell (NY: Random House, 1986), 78.

19 Leonard Cohen, "*Everybody Knows*," in *Stranger Music: Selected Poems and Songs* (Toronto: McClelland & Stewart, 1993), 361-362.

20 Merton, journal entry June 2, 1966, *Learning to Love*, 75.

21 Merton, journal entry June 3, 1966, *Learning to Love*, 77.

22 Merton, journal entry Sept. 2, 1966, *Learning to Love*, 119.

23 Merton, journal entry Sept. 4, 1966, *Learning to Love*, 124.

24 Merton, journal entry Sept. 26, 1966 where he quotes from a letter from M., *Learning to Love*, 145.

25   Merton, journal entry Sept. 18, 1959, *A Search for Solitude*, 330. Merton writes:
      "Have been reading a marvelous book of theology by the Orthodox Father Paul
      Evdokimov who teaches at Saint Serge in Paris. It is called *La femme et le salut
      due monde* [*Woman and the Salvation of the World*] but is in reality a whole survey
      of sophianic theology."

26   Merton, journal entry June 26, 1965, *Dancing in the Water of Life*, vol. 5, 1963-
      1965, ed. Robert E. Daggy (NY: HarperSanFrancisco, 1997), 260. See also Karl
      Stern's *The Flight from Woman* (NY: Farrar, Straus and Giroux, 1965).

27   Merton, journal entry Jan. 21, 1968, *The Other Side of the Mountain: The Journals
      of Thomas Merton*, Vol. 7: 1967-1968, ed. Patrick Hart (NY: HarperSanFrancisco,
      1999), 45. See also A. Riza Arasteh's *Final Integration in the Adult Personality*
      (Leiden, Netherlands: E.J. Brill, 1965).

28   Thomas Merton, "Final Integration: Toward a Monastic Therapy," in *Contempla-
      tion in a World of Action* (Notre Dame, Indiana: University of Notre Dame Press,
      1998), 157.

29   Merton, journal entry Aug. 20, 1968, *The Other Side of the Mountain*, 157.

30   Merton, journal entry Aug. 29, 1966, *Learning to Love*, 119.

31   Merton, journal entry May 20, 1966, *Learning to Love*, 67.

32   Paul Elie, *The Life You Save May Be Your Own: An American Pilgrimage* (Maryknoll,
      NY: Orbis Books, 2003). Elie writes, "A number of Merton's appointments in
      Louisville, that year [1966], were with a psychologist [James Wygal]. Now the
      psychologist arranged for Merton to have the use of the office when he was
      out. There, one afternoon in early summer, Merton and Margie met once
      more; there, they drank champagne and made love" (389). In a note to his
      biography Elie explains he had access to this information through an excised
      journal dated June 12, 1966 as "described in conversation by Robert Giroux"
      (523).

33   William Butler Yeats, "A Dialogue of Self and Soul," in *The Collected Poems of
      W.B. Yeats* (London MacMillan & Co. 1969), 267.

34   Merton, journal entry Sept. 6, 1966, *Learning to Love*, 126.

35   Merton, journal entry Sept. 21, 1966, *Learning to Love*, 140.

36   This line is an allusion to a line from Thomas Merton's "Untitled Poem"
      ("Paradise weeps in us") in *The Dark Before Dawn*, 191.

7.

Pivoting Toward Peace

The Transformative Poetry of
Thomas Merton and Denise Levertov

SUSAN MCCASLIN

In what way is poetry transformative? How can it pivot us toward peace, and to what extent? Both Denise Levertov (1923-1997) and Thomas Merton (1915-1968) grappled with these questions in their art and in their lives. On their respective journeys, neither poet abandoned the longing for an integral vision in which contemplation and action are unified. Both left a legacy of poetry that includes overtly political poems as well as more subtly lyrical and meditative ones that enact peace by offering glimpses of a world in which self and other are so deeply entwined that war makes no sense. In many of their most contemplative poems, the poem itself becomes an incarnation of the longing for justice and peace, a microcosm of ecological balance between inner and outer worlds. Another way of saying this is that the poem, poised between the interiority of the poet and the turmoil of the outer world, creates an alternative order, a place of high energy discharge that can bring about both individual and social transformation.

Though Merton found his religious vocation midway through his life and Levertov made her way to an ecumenical Catholic Christianity in the last decade of hers, the two poets share striking commonalities. Both became Americans after being born abroad (Levertov in England, Merton in France). Both were prolific prose and poetry writers, and both were drawn to the political poets of Latin America, though the influences on Merton's writing were more European and Levertov's more American. In addition, they eventually shared the same publisher in James Laughlin at New Directions.

Since the 1950s, Levertov had been associated with the Black Mountain school of poetics. Its alumni of American poets of the avant-garde included Robert Creeley, Ed Dorn, and Robert Duncan, all of whom were grounded in the free verse movement inspired by William Carlos Williams. Levertov's early neo-Romanticism had evolved into a poetry and poetics of political and social engagement by the time she published her collection of essays *The Poet in the World* in 1973.[1] Merton also gradually moved beyond his early renunciation of society and began to integrate social and political concerns into a more holistic vision.

Culturally rich and eclectic family heritages shaped both writers. Levertov's father was a Hasidic Russian Jew who converted to Christianity and became an Anglican priest, and her mother was Welsh and steeped in Celtic lore. Merton's parents were bohemian artists who roamed from place to place in Europe during his childhood. His father, Owen Merton, was from New Zealand, and his mother, Ruth Jenkins Merton, was an American Quaker who also had Celtic roots. Levertov writes of herself, "Among Jews a Goy, among Gentiles...a Jew..., among school children a strange exception whom they did not know whether to envy or mistrust: all of those anomalies predicated my later experience."[2] Merton lost both parents when young. He sought stability by joining the Abbey of Gethsemani in 1941 when he was 26, but remained intellectually expansive, as evidenced in his far-ranging correspondence and self-revelatory posthumously published journals. Levertov renounced organized religion for most of her life, converting to Catholicism later in her life in 1984 when she was 61. However, both poets were liminal writers with an outsider's sense of dwelling at the margins.

In addition to having family heritages that inspired their creativity, both poets set lyrical poems of deep interiority beside more engaged political poems. In fact, single poems often interweave both voices, which then become complementary since they stem from a unified base in experience. Levertov shifts from an early focus on mythopoetic themes to poems of more public concern; yet these two aspects of her work remain side by side throughout her canon. For instance, "A Tree Telling of Orpheus," where she retells the mythic story of Orpheus charming the creatures and trees, appears in the same 1966 volume as the political "A Marigold from North Vietnam."[3] In the latter, Levertov ponders the irony of how the soil from the roots of a marigold, once seen as a "resurrection flower," had been sent from Vietnam as a gift to a friend grieving the loss of a soldier who died there needlessly. The marigold becomes a symbol of both loss and the powers of regeneration.

Like Merton, Levertov argues that poets, as guardians of language, must take responsibility for the ethical impact of their words in the public sphere. In fact, her break with her mentor, poet Robert Duncan, was in part due to his resistance to her emerging political activism.[4] Both Merton and Levertov, then, stood as witnesses to injustice and spoke out publicly, whether through Merton's *Cold War Letters*, originally circulated in mimeographed form,[5] or Levertov's involvement in rallies and protests against the Vietnam War, nuclear testing in New Mexico, and the first Gulf War in Iraq. "Picket and pray" became her motto in her later years.

Both artists also explored a mystical-contemplative spirituality throughout their lives. Merton's dramatic conversion to Catholicism occurred in his mid-20s, but his faith passed through many metamorphoses. Though he lived most of his life at the monastery, his outward pilgrimages took him to places as diverse as Cuba, New York City, India, Sri Lanka, and Thailand. His concurrent inward pilgrimage led to engagement with other religions such as Sufism and Buddhism. In contrast, Levertov's Christian orientation emerged more gradually and flowered later in life. In her last essays, Levertov speaks of her journey as a pilgrimage. In 1991 she writes,

> But more and more, what I have sought as a *reading writer* is a poetry that, while it does not attempt to ignore or deny the ocean of crisis in which we swim, is itself 'on Pilgrimage,'...in search of significance underneath and beyond the succession of temporal events: a poetry which attests to [a] deep spiritual longing.[6]

While writing the poem "Mass for the Day of St. Thomas Didymus" (traditionally the doubting saint), she discovered she had moved unconsciously from observer to worshipper, for she states, "The experience of writing the poem – that long swim through waters of unknown depth – had been also a conversion process."[7] Though Levertov carved a longer trajectory toward Catholicism than Merton, the works of both writers trace the arc of a pilgrimage.

Given Merton and Levertov's shared spiritual and social passions and milieu, it seems inevitable that their lives should have intersected. Merton was reading Levertov in 1961 when he wrote to poet Ernesto Cardenal, "There is a very fine new poet, Denise Levertov. I forget whether you translated some of her work or not. She is splendid, one of the most promising."[8] In 1967, Levertov sent a letter to Merton requesting his written support for a Vietnam War protest, and he responded positively, initiating their short correspondence over matters political and poetic.

Merton and Levertov's first and only face-to-face encounter occurred on December 10, 1967 when she joined him and Kentucky poet Wendell Berry and his wife, Tanya, at the Abbey of Gethsemani. After her visit, Merton wrote in his journal,

> Rainy. Denise Levertov was here with Wendell Berry... They came up to the hermitage and spent the afternoon. I like Denise very much. A good warm person. She left a good poem ("Tenebrae") and we talked a little about Sister Norbert in San Francisco who is in trouble about protesting against the war.[9]

Merton's premature death outside Bangkok exactly one year later must have shocked Levertov, and it cut short a friendship that would surely have flourished. It is evident from her subsequent poems and prose writings that Merton remained a continuing influence and that he was a seminal influence in her movement toward Christianity. Her poem "On a Theme by Thomas Merton" (1992) reflects her ongoing respect for his work.[10] And her earlier 1984 remarks acknowledge him as one of the premier religious writers not only of her generation but of the ages.

> I see nothing detrimental to my own poetry in the fact that I participate in the Eucharist or that I read Julian of Norwich, Bonhoeffer, or Thomas Merton without skepticism. I am ecumenical to a degree no doubt scandalous to the more orthodox... [I]f I discover spiritual fellowship and an active commitment to my political values I take it where I find it.[11]

A number of Levertov's later, more explicitly religious poems echo or directly cite Merton, who becomes to her a kind of posthumous mentor. For instance, in *Breathing the Water* (1984),

Levertov's poem "I learned that her name was Proverb" is what she calls "a spinoff" of a line from Merton.[12] The source of the title, she writes in a note, "comes from the dream which Thomas Merton recounted in a letter to Boris Pasternak quoted in a review by Father Basil Pennington of Michael Mott's biography of Thomas Merton."[13] Levertov's note bears citing in order to indicate the depth of her serious study of Merton after his death. She was avidly following reviews, biographies, and correspondence related to him. As late as 1990 she invokes Merton as a model and inspiration for her growing faith. "If...a Thomas Merton...could believe, who was I to squirm and fret, as if I required more refined mental nourishment than [his]?"[14]

Levertov's note on her "spinoff" from Merton also reveals their shared fascination with the figure of Proverb-Sophia or Divine Wisdom (Hagia Sophia), which can be traced through Merton's journals, poems, and correspondence from 1958 when he wrote of his archetypal dream experience of Sophia-Wisdom. He comments, "I ask her name and she says her name is Proverb."[15] In the October 23, 1958 letter to Boris Pasternak that Levertov mentions, Merton clearly links his often-quoted experience of identifying with the divine in "ordinary" people at the corner of Fourth and Walnut in Louisville to this figure of Proverb.

> One night I dreamt that I was sitting with a very young Jewish girl of 14 or 15, and that she suddenly manifested a very deep and pure affection for me and embraced me so that I was moved to the depths of my soul. I learned that her name was "Proverb," which I thought very simple and beautiful... A few days later when I happened to be in a nearby city [Louisville]...I was walking alone in the crowded street and suddenly saw that everybody was Proverb and that in all of them shone her extraordinary beauty and purity and shyness, even though they did not know who

they were and were perhaps ashamed of their names –
because they were mocked on account of them. And they
did not know their real identity as the Child so dear to God
who, from before the beginning, was playing in His sight all
days, playing in the world.[16]

Merton and Levertov's common focus on the figure of Wisdom
is connected to their shared image of God as a feminine presence of peace and mercy in the world.

Before Levertov embraced the Christian mystical, sophianic
traditions and an intentional spiritual practice of her own, she
struggled with the question of whether or not a poetry of peace
is even possible in times of violence. In her "Poetry and Peace,"
an address at a conference at Stanford in 1989 on the theme of
"Women, War, and Peace," Levertov was confronted with a question from the audience proposing that poets should bring images of peace to the world.[17] Her continuing rumination over
this question led to the following poem, entitled "Making Peace."

A voice from the dark called out,
"The poets must give us
imagination of peace, to oust the intense, familiar
imagination of disaster. Peace, not only
the absence of war."
                    But peace, like a poem,
is not there ahead of itself,
can't be imagined before it is made,
can't be known except
in the words of its making,
grammar of justice,
syntax of mutual aid...
                    A line of peace might appear
if we restructured the sentence our lives are making,
revoked its reaffirmation of profit and power,

questioned our needs, allowed
long pauses...
          A cadence of peace might balance its weight
on that different fulcrum; peace, a presence,
an energy field more intense than war,
a mighty pulse then,
stanza by stanza into the world,
each act of living
one of its words, each word
a vibration of light — facets
of the forming crystal.[18]

Peace is "not there ahead of itself" because for Levertov it must be forged in the alembic of our lives. True peace is not a quietist state but one that emerges from an inner silence that leads to action. Therefore, if a poet writes words that call for personal and collective transformation, the poet herself must be willing to get involved and put herself, not just her work, on the line. She writes, "When words penetrate deep into us they change the chemistry of the soul, of the imagination. We have no right to do that to people if we don't share the consequences."[19]

    Poets who share these political consequences, forging what Levertov called "engaged" poems, and entering the arena of activism, must also be careful, according to Levertov, not to fall into the didactic. She was aware of how assuming a public voice can often lead poets into polemic or propaganda.

Good poets write bad political poems only if they let themselves write deliberate, opinionated, rhetoric, misusing their art as propaganda. The poet does not *use* poetry, but is at the service of poetry. To *use* it is to *misuse* it. A poet driven to speak to himself, to maintain a dialogue with himself, concerning politics, can expect to write as well upon that theme as upon any other. He cannot separate it from everything else in his life. But it is not whether or not good "political" poems are a possibility that is in question. What is in question is the role of the poet as observer or as participant in the life of his time.[20]

She responds to the question of whether political poetry can be truly poetic in "Poetry, Prophecy, Survival."

A poetry of anguish, a poetry of anger, of rage, a poetry that, from literal or deeply imagined experience, depicts and denounces perennial injustice and cruelty in their current forms, and in our peculiar time warns of the unprecedented perils that confront us, can be truly a high poetry, as well wrought as any other.[21]

Her response is that poetry that rages against injustice is a "high poetry" if it is highly evocative, well-crafted, and emerges from the life experience of the artist.

Levertov also remarks on why art (and particularly poetry) is so effective as a catalyst for peace in her essay "Paradox and Equilibrium" (1988).

We humans cannot absorb the bitter truths of our own history, the revelation of our destructive potential, except through the mediation of art (the manifestation of our other, our constructive potential). Presented raw, the facts are rejected: perhaps not by the intellect, which accommodates them as statistics, but by the emotions – which hold the key to conscience and resolve.[22]

Here she argues that poetry can be more effective than discursive prose because it emerges from the depths of the soul and transforms raw emotions through the fires of the creative imagination. Art, she suggests, allows us to look on our own destructive potential without despair, awakening our capacity to first acknowledge evil and injustice in ourselves and in the world, and then "muster the will to transcend it."[23]

Both Merton and Levertov crafted poems that speak to resisting injustice. Many of these are commentaries on particular historical events. Such poems draw on the devices of irony, satire, and parody, which are often associated with the Hebraic prophetic voice of rage and denunciation. Levertov's poem "An Interim" is a call for imaginative attention and empathy with the suffering of others. That which is witnessed compels moral response.

> But we need
> the few who could bear no more,
> who would try anything,
> who would take the chance
> that their deaths among the uncountable
> masses of dead might be real to those who
> don't dare imagine death.
> Might burn through the veil that blinds
> those who do not imagine the burned bodies
> of other people's children.[24]

She associates this stance with that of the prophets of ancient Israel.

> And this brings one to a very important factor which is
> shared by poets and prophets: prophetic utterance, like
> poetic utterance, transforms experience and moves the
> received to new attitudes...We also need direct images in
> our art that will waken, warn, stir their hearers to action;
> images that will both appall and empower.[25]

Merton's similarly political poem "Chant to Be Used in Processions around a Site with Furnaces" (from *Emblems of a Season of Fury*, 1963) is an example of a prophetic poem that both "appall[s] and empower[s]" in Levertov's sense. It uses corrosive irony, startling juxtapositions, understatement, and a flat, dehumanized tone to lay open the inner workings of the bureaucratic mind and its complicity with systemic evil.

> How we made them sleep and purified them
> How we perfectly cleaned up the people and worked a big
> heater
> I was the commander I made improvements and installed a
> guaranteed system
> taking account of human weakness I purified
> and I remained decent
> How I commanded
> I made cleaning appointments and then I made the
> travelers sleep
> and after that I made soap.[26]

Merton's anti-chant is chilling because it uses a Nazi war criminal persona, the language of mechanization and abstraction, passive voice, and euphemism ("sleep" for "die"). The speaker's self-absorption (repeated use of "I") and delusional thinking ("I did my rightful duty as commanded") plunge the reader into a clinical hell. The poem reminds us of how easily we can dehumanize ourselves if we give ourselves over to a system that would dehumanize others. Yet the poem simultaneously empowers us to maintain an inner vigilance against such a moral descent.

During the Cold War, both Merton and Levertov wrote compellingly on the implications of what Hannah Arendt called "the banality of evil" in the context of the Eichmann trials. Both were critical of the war-hungry bureaucracies in the States that kept alive the hatred of "the other" in the name of resisting

Communism. Levertov wrote a poem called "During the Eichmann Trial" (from *The Jacob's Ladder*, 1961) which employs the figure of Eichmann to speak to the potential in each of us for betrayal of our common humanity.

> He stands isolate in a bulletproof
> witness-stand of glass,
> a cage, where we may view
> ourselves, an apparition[27]

Much later, in the 1990s, Levertov demonstrates another strategy. Her "Witnessing from Afar the New Escalation of Savage Power" offers a poetic-political experience of the effects of the first Gulf War. The poem depicts the devastation in one woman's life due to a bombing raid, and compels engagement with her suffering. Its well-wrought lines shock the reader yet avoid mere rant.

> There was a crash and throb
> of harsh sound audible
> always, but distant.
> She believed
> she had it in her
> to fend for herself and hold
> despair at bay.
> Now when she came to the ridge and saw
> the world's raw gash
> reopened, the whole world
> a valley of steaming blood,
> her small wisdom
> guttered in the uprush;
> *rubbledust, meatpulse*—
> darkness and the blast
> levelled her.[28]

We are told that the elderly woman had "tended a small altar, / kept a candle shielded there," but could not ward off through her simple faith the violence brought about by human hate. The stunning image of the "world's raw gash" reminds us that "the whole world" is affected by the "leveling" that crushes the spirit in all.

Such poems open new ways of witnessing, imagining others' pain. Seeing deeply can lead to empathy or compassion; compassion to transformed ways of being in the world. If witnessing from within compels action, then Merton and Levertov's explicitly political poems need to be revived in the context of our current global conflicts. Their engaged political poems disturb us, while the more contemplative poems gently pivot us toward peace by pointing to another way of being in the world that, if enacted in many, could lead to social transformation.

Both Merton and Levertov composed their more subtle peace poems by drawing from the natural world to enact a shift in perception. Their legacy is a poetic of praise through a contemplative vision of the world. In *Contemplation in a World of Action*, Merton writes,

> The contemplative life should liberate and purify the
> imagination which passively absorbs all kinds of things
> without our realizing it; liberate and purify it from the
> influence of so much violence done by the bombardment of
> social images.[29]

Contemplative poetry counters the bombardments of the culture – its abuses of language, its steady onslaught of advertising and propaganda that turns us into thoughtless consumers and makes us complicit in the machinery of war. Reading poetry can become an act of contemplative attention that evokes contemplative states in its hearers and readers. As Levertov insists, the more celebratory sort of peace poem offers a counterbalance to the poems of outrage.

But we need also the poetry of praise, of love for the world, the vision of the potential for good even in our species which has so messed up the rest of creation, so fouled its own nest. If we lose the sense of contrast, of the opposites to all the grime and gore, the torture, the banality of the computerized apocalypse, we lose the reason for trying to work for redemptive change... To sing awe to breathe out praise and celebration – is as fundamental an impulse as to lament.[30]

Ultimately, these twin poles of the prophetic and the celebratory coexist in an authentic poetic of peace. Some poems emphasize the outrage and others the praise, while others encompass the two in a single poem. The peace poetry of Levertov and Merton is poetry of ecological awareness in the largest sense. That is, if ecology is the study of how all things are interconnected and part and parcel of a larger, purposive, and therefore sacred whole, then a poetry and poetic that enters this unified field with contemplative attention is one that might bring healing to the broken collective psyche. In one way, all poetry that raises consciousness past dualistic either/or, them/us thinking is peace poetry. Such poetry is inherently ecological because it keeps us from seeing our fellow humans or the natural world as resources to be exploited or objectified. It grounds us in community and in the cosmos or larger order of things. True peace poetry leads to a de-centering of ego and an encounter with a more authentic and expansive self. Such poetry is essential because it gives us more than notions and concepts.

In her last years, when she lived near Seattle, Levertov spoke of a Northwestern poetry of wilderness that "gives rise to a more conscious attentiveness to the non-human and to a more or less conscious desire to immerse the self in that larger whole."[31] She found herself drawn to poems that "approach spiritual longing and spiritual experience in a way that is more direct, since it is frankly about the quest for or the encounter with God."[32]

Two astonishingly beautiful ecological/spiritual peace poems are Merton's "Night-Flowering Cactus"[33] and Levertov's "To Live in the Mercy of God."[34] Both identify with the flood of beauty and love that is the divine Oneness manifesting in and through humans and the natural world. Both poets recognize the complex mystery of nature, how it can be an expression of clashing powers striving for survival as well as a unified ground of being. In their most mystical nature poems, they focus on this spiritual dimension of nature. In Merton's poem, spirit manifests from a point of nothingness within a cactus that blooms only one night each year.

I know my time, which is obscure, silent, and brief
For I am present without warning one night only...

When I come I lift my sudden Eucharist?
Out of the earth's unfathomable joy
Clean and total I obey the world's body
I am intricate and whole, not art but wrought passion
Excellent deep pleasure of essential waters
Holiness of form and mineral mirth:

I am the extreme purity of virginal thirst...

He who sees my purity
Dares not speak of it.
When I open once for all my impeccable bell
No one questions my silence:
The all-knowing bird of night flies out of my mouth.

Have you seen it? Then though my mirth has quickly ended
You live forever in its echo:
You will never be the same again.[35]

This is one of Merton's most deeply mystical poems, for it voices both the inner gnosis of the mortal, individual poet as well as the divine feminine presence and principle immanent in the world. The night-flowering cactus emerges from the virgin point of nothingness within the holy ground of silence beyond all our categories and utters her beauty from the depths "clean and total." To identify even for an instant with this sacramental grace is to participate in a timeless unity where there is no more war within the self. The listener is not merely accosted by purity but invited to be "the extreme purity of virginal thirst," which is longing for union with the absolute. The sacramental emphasis on nature as "Eucharist" suggests that the human soul and the natural world, when perceived from this awareness, are a theophany or manifestation of the divine. Like Rilke's famous poem "Archaic Torso of Apollo,"[36] which ends, "You must change your life," the conclusion of Merton's poem calls forth in the reader a transformation that is at once moral, emotional, rational, sensual, and spiritual.

Similarly, in Levertov's "To Live in the Mercy of God,"[37] a waterfall pouring through a west coast rain forest becomes a metaphor for the divine mercy.

> To live in the mercy of God.
>
> To feel vibrate the enraptured
> waterfall flinging itself
> unabating down and down
>   to clenched fists of rock.
> Swiftness of plunge,
> hour after year after century,
>   O or Ah
> uninterrupted, voice
> many-stranded.
>   To breathe
> spray. The smoke of it.

> Arcs
> of steelwhite foam, glissades
> of fugitive jade barely perceptible. Such passion —
> rage or joy?
>   Thus, not mild, not temperate,
> God's love for the world. Vast
> flood of mercy
>   flung on resistance.[38]

These last lines seem a deliberate echo of Merton's words spoken as the "Voice of God" at the end of *The Sign of Jonas*.

> I have always overshadowed Jonas with My mercy, and
> cruelty I know not at all. Have you had sight of Me, Jonas My
> child? Mercy within mercy within mercy.[39]

Levertov's late poem on divine mercy likewise establishes the Eros of the divine as it woos its recalcitrant human creation. The issue in both poems is whether we choose to open ourselves or resist the flow of mercy. But whether they speak out against injustice or open silently to grace, the contemplative poems of Merton and Levertov can move us toward peace. Indeed, in the work of these two significant religious poets of the mid-to-late 20th century, the simultaneous opening to the spirit and resistance to injustice are twin aspects of a single motion.

1   Denise Levertov, *The Poet in the World* (New York: New Directions, 1973).
2   Denise Levertov, "Autobiographical Sketch," in *Denise Levertov: New & Selected Essays* (New York: New Directions, 1992), 260.
3   Denise Levertov, *Relearning the Alphabet* (New York: New Directions, 1966) 81, 67.
4   See *The Letters of Robert Duncan and Denise Levertov*, ed. Robert J. Bertholf and Albert Gelpi (Stanford, CA: Stanford University Press, 2004). The breach between Levertov and Duncan was complex, but in part the result of Duncan's public criticism of Levertov's political activism during the Vietnam War. The correspondence between them suggests that he felt her political engagement against the war in both writings and acts (protests, rallies, etc.) was shrill, and compromised her integrity as an artist.

5   Thomas Merton, *Cold War Letters*, ed. William H. Shannon and Christine M. Bochen (Maryknoll, NY: Orbis, 2006).

6   Levertov, "Some Affinities of Content," in *Essays*, 4.

7   Levertov, "Work That Enfaiths," in *Essays*, 249. This poem first appeared in *Candles in Babylon* (New York: New Directions, 1982). It reappears in *Denise Levertov: Selected Poems*, ed. Paul A. Lacey; Preface Robert Creeley (New York: New Directions, 2002), 130.

8   Thomas Merton, *The Courage for Truth: Letters to Writers*, ed. Christine M. Bochen (New York: Farrar, Straus, Giroux, 1993), 127.

9   Thomas Merton, *The Other Side of the Mountain: The Journals of Thomas Merton*, Vol. 7: 1967-1968, ed. Patrick Hart (San Francisco: HarperCollins, 1998), 22.

10   Denise Levertov, *Evening Train* (New York: New Directions, 1992), 113.

11   Denise Levertov, "A Poet's View," *Essays*, 244.

12   Denise Levertov, *Breathing the Water* (New York: New Directions, 1987), 51. Levertov in a note defines a "spinoff" as "a verbal construct which neither describes nor comments but moves off at a tangent to, or parallel with, its inspiration" (85-86).

13   Ibid., 85.

14   Levertov, "Work that Enfaiths," *Essays*, 250-51.

15   Thomas Merton, *A Search for Solitude: The Journals of Thomas Merton*, Vol.3: 1952-1960, ed. Lawrence S. Cunningham (San Francisco: HarperCollins, 1996), 176.

16   Merton, *The Courage for Truth*, 90.

17   Levertov, "Poetry and Peace: Some Broader Definitions," *Essays*, 154.

18   Denise Levertov, *Making Peace*, ed. Peggy Rosenthal (New York: New Directions, 2006), 58.

19   Levertov, "The Poet in the World," in *Essays*, 136.

20   Ibid., 136-137.

21   Levertov, "Poetry, Prophecy, Survival," *Essays*, 143-44. Variants of this piece were presented orally on two or three different occasions in the early 1980s.

22   Ibid., 141.

23   Ibid., 142.

24   Denise Levertov, *Poems 1968-1972* (New York: New Directions, 1987), 26.

25   Levertov, *Essays*, 148-149.

26   Thomas Merton, *The Collected Poems of Thomas Merton* (NY: New Directions, 1977), 345-346.

27   Denise Levertov, in *Denise Levertov: Poems 1960-1967* (New York: New Directions, 1966), 65.

28   Levertov, *Evening Train*, 80.

29   Thomas Merton, *Contemplation in a World of Action* (Garden City, NY: Doubleday, 1971), 230.

30   Levertov, *Essays*, 144.

31   Levertov, "Some Affinities of Content," *Essays*, 6.

32   Levertov, *Essays*, 11.

33   Merton, *Collected Poems*, 351-352.

34   Levertov, *Sands of the Well* (New York: New Directions, 1996), 127-128.

35   Merton, *Collected Poems*, 351-352.

36   Rainer Maria Rilke, trans. C. F. MacIntyre, *Rilke: Selected Poems* (Univ. of California Press, 1957). Merton most often used the MacIntyre translation.

37   Levertov, *Sands of the Well*, 127.

38   Ibid., 127-128.

39   Merton, *The Sign of Jonas* (New York: Harcourt, Brace, 1953), 362.

Sophia Awakening Merton, the Trees, and Me

SUSAN MCCASLIN

A tree gives glory to God by being a tree.
— Thomas Merton, *New Seeds of Contemplation*

I exist under trees. I walk in the woods out of necessity...
I share this particular place with them: we form an
ecological balance.
— Thomas Merton, *Day of a Stranger*

What Will This Woman Do?

When I retired after 38 years of teaching English and creative writing, I had some serious internal conversations centered on the perennial question, *Who am I?* Who am I beyond my constructed self, my roles as poet, educator, wife, mother, etc.? Who or what might I become?

I began to reflect on Merton's notions about the true versus the false self, the ego versus our deeper, essential self that is grounded in unitive being, the part of us interconnected with the community, the planet, and the cosmic order of things. What might it take to sustain that balance between contemplation and action of which Merton so eloquently spoke? "The problem of sanctity and salvation is in fact the problem of finding out who I truly am and of discovering my truest self, my essence or core," says Merton.[1]

More specifically, I wondered if, as an introverted poet entranced with reading, reflection, and writing, I might become more politically engaged. As a young woman, I had marched in the streets against the war in Vietnam, and later, even with a child and a full-time vocation, I continued to take an interest in the public domain, writing occasional letters about political issues. Since childhood I had been bookish and knew from the age of 12 that I wanted to be a poet. As I matured, I came to see writing as my chosen form of peaceful activism, and so it remains.

Balancing the lyrical and exploratory voice with a poetics of political engagement was challenging. Merton's words in *Contemplation in a World of Action* have served as a guide.

> In the contemplative life, action exists for the sake of contemplation and vice versa. The openness of the contemplative is justified insofar as it enables [her] to be a better contemplative and to share with others the fruit of [her] contemplation.[2]

Yet it seemed Sophia had something else in mind for me after I turned 60, something surprising and much larger than I had imagined. My husband Mark and I joined energies in an environmental activist campaign. As Sophia appeared to Merton, so she appeared to me in a visionary dream as an awakener, rousing me from sleep and sending me out on the road.

> I am awakened, I am born again at the voice of this my
> Sister, sent to me from the depths of the divine fecundity.
> – Thomas Merton, "Hagia Sophia"[3]

A Dream of Sophia, Activator [4]

There is in all visible things an invisible fecundity, a dimmed
light, a meek namelessness, a hidden wholeness.
–Thomas Merton, "Hagia Sophia"

Just one year into retirement, I had a vivid dream experience of
being in an Arctic landscape. I found myself travelling through
ice fields and past snow-covered mountains under azure skies.
Pools of glacial-blue intensity dotted the landscape stretching
before me. Steam rose from their surfaces, and they beckoned
from a distance – hot springs, geothermal dazzlers, warm eyes
gazing up out of the permafrost.

A group of us, tourists and pilgrims, had made its way from
a log lodge and hiked across the snowfields to a grotto where
we found the first of the pools. I removed my backpack, parka,
clothing, and boots and plunged naked into its welcoming
warmth. The waters relaxed yet invigorated me, melting away
what seemed like decades of stress. After a day exploring a few
more of these hot spring grottos, I dressed and made my way
back toward the lodge. As I entered the building, I noticed a
side door that led to a small room where it was whispered a
wise woman was "telling fortunes." Curious, I waited in line for
my turn to receive a few words from the sage.

I stepped into an unadorned room with no furnishings.
Nothing hung on the white walls. At one end of the room in a
far corner I saw a very aged woman who resembled my long-
deceased friend Olga, a woman who for 16 years had been my
spiritual mentor. The woman was lying on the floor on a pallet
or stretcher and it appeared she was dying. Her eyes were the
exact shade of blue as the pools. She was clearly a living embodiment of the Arctic landscape, white-headed but with sap-
phire eyes. She signaled me to kneel beside her bed and tell my
story.

I did, pouring out all my cares, relating how I had recently retired and was feeling lost, uncertain whether to write another book, study French, offer a workshop on the mystics, or travel to Turkey. I confessed in tears how I was having trouble reinventing myself, and that I felt like a failure. Then I blurted out how I was also feeling my age – *61* – and had new aches and pains, the start of arthritis, a back problem, some grey hairs. Through all my babbling, she remained silent, absorbing and holding a space for my confusion, shame, grief, and fear. I had never experienced such absolute, non-judgmental attention.

Yet as I spoke again of aging, she unexpectedly threw back her head in a long laugh. At first, I assumed she was laughing *at* me and I felt embarrassed; then I realized it was absurd that I should be telling this Ancient of Days how very old I felt. From her perspective, I was a child. As I noticed her creased face, the face of the oldest person I had ever seen, I grasped the absurdity of my whining and started to laugh too, for her laughter, a compelling outburst of sheer, unadulterated joy, was infectious.

Finally, I stopped laughing and awaited a word from her, my Sophia, Mother, and Friend. For I was suddenly aware this being before whom I was kneeling was not merely Olga, but absolute Being, Becoming, beyond all dualities, God, the Goddess, the whole of the wide universe, compressed into the form of a very old woman.

> This is at once my own being, my own nature, and the Gift
> of my Creator's Thought and Art within me, speaking as
> Hagia Sophia, speaking as my sister Wisdom.
> – Thomas Merton, "Hagia Sophia"[5]

Then she bent forward, clasped my hands, locked her eyes with mine, and enunciated slowly, "BE BOLD!" As I was yanked out of the visionary state, I asked, "Who is this woman?" and a voice reverberated three times, "Sophia, Sophia, Sophia."

Bold! In that moment of her speaking, radiance played in her face and made her seem young. Being bold seemed the most natural thing in the world. The stretcher or deathbed was more like a maternity bed. There was no more for her to say or for me to receive.

At first, I had the impression the figure in the vision was Olga; yet on leaving the dream I was told she represented Sophia. Clearly, Olga was and remained a Sophia or wisdom figure for me; yet the aged one of my dream was archetypal. Now I see how both the personal and transpersonal co-inhere. The figure in the dream was both Olga and an embodiment of Holy Wisdom.

> I am awakened. I am born again at the voice of this my
> Sister, sent to me from the depths of the divine fecundity.
> — Thomas Merton, "Hagia Sophia"[6]

Bold. The short, crisp, West Saxon word contains the word "old" but is not limited by it. It is stark, a spitfire utterance reminding one of a Viking conqueror, but it clearly applies to the spiritual realms. Did Sophia mean "bold" like the Arctic landscape itself, deep blue contrasted to gelid white? Or bold like fire and ice, containing a union of opposites? Or bold like a mother who has cast off the kind of mothering I felt was expected of me for some new mode of being? Through the encounter with Sophia I remain emboldened.

Reading recent reports of melting icecaps and the shifting of the poles, I see too that Arctic Sophia's message is pragmatic and political. It is a call to address the impacts on the earth of human technological development and unsustainable consumption. It is not at all surprising that such inner experiences resonate at both the personal and the socio-political levels.

Here's one way of reading the vision: the ancient earth mother is sick and dying because of the activities of humans.

She is calling us to join her in the work of earth restoration. She will survive, but *we* may not unless we join with her in the bold work of repairing what we have damaged. I did not know it at the time, but a few years later I would be drawn into an environmental cause related to the saving of a local rainforest in my neighborhood. The poetry I was soon to write would increasingly concern itself with our endangered global ecosystems. I would be getting bolder.

The Han Shan Poetry Initiative[7]

Trees and animals have no problem. God makes them what they are without consulting them, and they are perfectly satisfied.
–Thomas Merton, *New Seeds of Contemplation*

Since childhood, my husband has been inspired by the beauty and mysteries of nature. He, like Merton in the following poem, experienced the emergence of a deer from the woods as an epiphany.

After thrashing in the water of the reservoir
The deer swims beautifully
And so escapes
Limping across the country into the little cedars....
Yes they can kill
The lovely doe and deer
In and out of season....

But he sees again
The curved and graceful deer
Fighting in the water
And then leaving
– from "Merlin and the Deer"[8]

Out of the desire to protect a local region where he had camped and explored as a boy, an area filled with wildlife, my husband became a committed environmental activist in his early 30s. After discovering this beloved valley near Coquitlam, British Columbia was endangered by proposed logging and development, he and others lobbied the BC government in what became a successful grassroots campaign to save 38,000 hectares of mountains, valleys, and old growth forest. This area, where he took me for hikes to waterfalls and lakes when we were first falling in love in 1978, is now officially protected as Pinecone Burke Provincial Park.

Eventually, my husband decided to become an environmental lawyer. He worked for a variety of non-profit societies for decades, and later taught environmental law and worked with students at the University of Victoria's Environmental Law Clinic. I supported his efforts from the start and often thought that while he was serving as a peaceful eco-hero, my more hidden work was to deepen into poetry and the writing life, which always seemed to flow along compatibly with my career as an educator. So we supported each other in our separate but complementary endeavours. I sometimes envisioned us as a microcosm of what William Blake called "the contraries" – complementary opposites.

Mark and I now reside in Glen Valley, a rural area in the Fraser Valley just east of Fort Langley, British Columbia. On Thanksgiving Day of 2012, we visited a 25-acre mature rainforest just a few kilometres from our home. We had heard the Township of Langley was planning to sell it off to raise capital funds to build a recreation centre in a neighbouring community.

As we strolled under the canopy of Douglas fir, Western redcedar, and hemlock, the light filtered down on us through the branches. We stepped over maidenhair, sword, and liquorice ferns, then paused at the base of a giant Black Cottonwood, a tree said to be hundreds of years old. I knew that this was it. I'd fallen in love with a forest and become an activist. I would drop everything and do whatever it might take to help save this particular forest.

We soon discovered that this land and a neighbouring parcel had been public land for many decades. The westernmost parcel, known to locals then as McLellan Forest, had been taken off the market because of a public outcry led by a local group of residents calling themselves WOLF (Watchers of Langley Forests). However, the easternmost forest was slated to be sold immediately. These same conservationists appealed once again to the Township, and the mayor and councillors gave WOLF a two-month window in which to raise three million dollars to purchase the second parcel of land. Time would run out on December 17.

This handful of people without extensive experience in fundraising wasn't having much success in coming up with the money. Many locals felt it was unfair to force residents to buy back land already belonging to them. Besides, shouldn't there be other ways for the Township to raise funds for capital projects rather than destroying a rare, wild ecosystem of lasting heritage value?

We later discovered that a developer was waiting in the wings with a signed offer. He planned to purchase the land, selectively log it, and then build private country estates, likely retaining some of the older trees. It would cease to be a vital ecosystem providing suitable habit for several rare or at-risk species, including the Pacific Water Shrew, Oregon Spotted Frog, Red-legged Frog, and Great Blue Heron. And the land would no longer be accessible to the public.

A local biologist and an environmental studies professor from a nearby university had documented the rarity and ecological value of the forested area, but the mayor and the majority of the councillors continued to speak of the land as "inventory," "surplus," and "idle land." A public outcry had already begun; experts had spoken at Township meetings and concerned residents were writing in to the local newspapers.

It takes a village to save a rainforest. But what might an artist do? I began remembering some successful unions of art and activism. In 1989, visual artists created paintings of the Carmanah Valley on Vancouver Island to raise awareness about the proposed logging of old growth forests there. Deep ecologists like American poet W.S. Merwin and conservationist farmer Wendell Berry had written poems that celebrated the intrinsic value of wild habitats in the US. Poets often realize how much we require nature and other species in order to be fully human, or to *be* at all, for we too are "nature" and are sustained by these fragile ecosystems. Therefore, I decided my contribution would be to organize "An Afternoon of Art and Activism" in the forest.

This event drew together local visual artists, poets, musicians, ecologists, photographers, a dancer, university students, high school students, and the general public of all ages. We set up tents under the widely-spaced trees and provided refreshments and information about the history and ecological value of the land. Poets read their tree poems, student played violins and guitars and sang, the dancer danced, and people paused to absorb the beauty of the forest. A local environmentalist from the Western Canada Wilderness Committee gave an inspiring speech and later made a short documentary of the day. Local newspaper reporters arrived and the event was covered in the local press.

A week later, 160 high school students on a field trip from the nearby Langley School of Fine Arts poured out of two big yellow buses to sketch, sing, and photograph the forest. After sharing their art in the woods, the students organized a poetry reading and photo exhibition at a local café. Several of them produced a short documentary film as a school project.

But the campaign wasn't over. My husband happened to notice an ad in the local paper announcing a book signing by esteemed Canadian wildlife artist Robert Bateman in a nearby mall. On a whim, he emailed Bateman's website, and a few hours later Bateman himself responded by phone: "Yes, I'll be there first thing in the morning." When he arrived, we thanked him profusely for rearranging his schedule, but all he said was, "This is important!" He indicated that for a long time he had come to see raising consciousness about local ecological issues as his primary purpose. Getting children and artists into the natural world was his particular mission. At one point, Bateman commented on the irony of logging a vital ecosystem in order to build a recreation centre elsewhere. "This is the recreation centre, right here!" He underscored the remark by gesturing to the earth with his thumbs. My writer and poet friends were encouraging and eloquent in their support for protection. Dispersed across Canada, many would be unlikely to come see the forest for themselves. I wondered how their voices could be present.

Then I recalled how as an undergraduate I had taken a course in ancient Chinese literature and studied the zesty poems of an old hermit monk named Han Shan, who is said to have lived on Cold Mountain during the Tang Dynasty around the 9th century C.E. Legend has it that he scribbled poems on rocks and suspended them from trees. It seemed appropriate to me that a Chinese poet might inspire a new poetry initiative on the west coast of BC because Gary Snyder, an American poet popular in the late 1960s, saw Han Shan as a Pacific Rim figure. Poetry is timeless, and Han Shan was to become my forest mentor and muse.

The young lover Orlando in *A Midsummer Nights Dream* placed poems for Rosalind on trees in the Forest of Arden. Poets have often written about trees, and world trees figure in many of our global mythologies and spiritual traditions. My own experience as a child singing in an apple tree rose up before me. The Han Shan Poetry Project was born.

I put out a call for tree poems on the websites of the various writers' organizations to which I belong. Soon my calls were appearing on people's blogs and websites all over the world. Over

150 poems poured in within a week and a half, and within two weeks the number surpassed 200. My husband and I, with the help of WOLF, sealed the poems in plastic paper protectors, threaded them with colourful ribbon, and spent an afternoon festooning them on trees without harming a single branch.

Poems continued pouring in from across British Columbia and other provinces in Canada, as well as from New Mexico, California, Florida, the UK, Australia, and Turkey. The contributions included poems from major award-winning Canadian poets such as Lorna Crozier, Patrick Lane, and Fred Wah (then Poet Laureate of Canada), as well as poems from established writers, beginning writers, and children as young as six years of age.

The forest wanted to be democratic, embracing all types of artistry, accomplishments, and styles. Fluttering against the emerald drapery, poems pirouetted like white angels. Rain and frost seemed to us the forest's way of reclaiming our human offerings. Or were the poems protecting the trees? We advertised the event in the local papers as the forest's anthology, the forest's art installation, where poets set their small gestures of creative expression beside the older and more primal creativity of nature. It seemed to me paradoxical that an apparently "soft" form like poetry could hold such fiercely tender power.

People were moved and came from all over to walk through the woods, pausing to read poems against a background of the sounds of the Northwestern Crow, Varied Thrush, and Downy Woodpecker. Soon articles on this project appeared in newspapers, magazines, and media outlets across Canada. My daughter's friends in Quebec saw her on the national news speaking about the forest.

One poet brought her companion to photograph her beside the tree where her poem fluttered. Suddenly he dropped to his knees, drew a ring out of his pocket, and proposed marriage. I was their guide through the forest; so at their request I pulled out my camera to memorialize the occasion.

The diversity of the art forms that manifested at the call of the forest is striking. Local visual artist Susan J. Falk created a series of 13 paintings inspired by the Han Shan poems and by her own meanderings in the forest. Later, she held an exhibition and silent auction and donated the proceeds from the sale of her works to WOLF. The Langley Opus Women's Choir performed in the forest just before Christmas.

At a Langley Township meeting just prior to the December 17 deadline, WOLF informed the mayor and council that their organization was not able to raise the required three million dollars. My husband then produced a letter he had received that afternoon from the BC Ministry of Environment saying that, in response to its own ecological assessment, the area should be protected as an "ecological reserve." One councillor quickly asked if the Ministry was willing to provide any funds to make this happen and was told, "Not at this time."

"Well, as they say in the business," the politician retorted while rubbing his fingers together, "show me the money."

Yet as a result of the new scientific reports and unrelenting media attention, the mayor and council met *in camera* after the public meeting and announced a few days later that the forest had been given another reprieve until January 21. In late December, *The Langley Advance* declared the McLellan Forest issue the "story of the year."

The Han Shan Poetry Initiative continued to garner press and visitors though the holiday season, but on January 22, 2013 we decided it was time for the poems to come down. Had I continued to send out calls for poems, the display could have grown and remained up much longer, but we felt the initiative had run its course. So the forest again spoke for itself without human signage. The removal of the poems was ceremonious, leaving a clean-swept feeling. Afterward, I noticed how frost coated the branches in the crisp air. The title of poet Don Domanski's tree poem sang in my ears: "Biodiversity is the mother of all beauty."

On January 28, after another closed meeting, the mayor and council sent out a press release stating they had determined to take the parcels in the western part of the forest off the market while authorizing the sale of three lots to the east. We were enormously relieved that the union of art and activism had resulted in rescuing 60% of the forest. But our elation was mixed with disappointment, since the portion of land the politicians wished to sell contained some of the most sensitive habitat for species-at-risk. What they presented as a rational compromise seemed to us a dividing of the baby. But we knew that without the media attention and public outcry they would surely have sold the entire forest.

The story was not over. As a result of all the media attention, a local farmer's widow, Mrs. Ann Blaauw, stepped forward to purchase the land in its entirety as a legacy in honour of her late husband Thomas Blaauw. She and Tom were farmers who loved the forest, and in their younger years used to picnic there. With the support of her family, Mrs. Blaauw purchased the entirety of the forest for over $2.5 million, then donated it to the nearby Trinity Western University to be maintained as a research forest and ecological preserve. My husband helped ensure that restrictive covenants were put in place and public access maintained. Now renamed the Blaauw Eco Forest, the area is managed by TWU's Environmental Studies Department, and students are carrying out important species inventories.

As the months of intense activity subsided, one part of me longed to return to writing in seclusion. The forest had already blessed me with a number of poems and I wanted to return to the writing process. Yet this beautiful union of ecology and poetry – eco-poetry – demonstrates how contemplation and action can dovetail in unaccountable ways.

Certainly, the arts have an untapped potential for transforming society. Perhaps this is because art can lead us to pause before beauty and thus alter how we see. It has the capacity to lift us past our short-term, self-serving ends. It appeals to a common recognition of beauty in biodiversity, transcending ideologies and polemic. Both authentic art and nature draw us into a realm of exchange not based merely on capital or profit, but on gift-gifting and receiving in another kind of economy, that of membership in a common household. This is perhaps why the Romantic poet William Blake called on every man and every woman to become an artist in the sense of exercising the creative imagination in some way.

I have friends who have plunged into unions of art and activism in their local areas without having such a positive outcome as we were privileged to enjoy. When I leapt into the fray of months of lobbying, writing, speaking at Township meetings, and arranging media contacts, there were many times when I had to face what seemed the certainty that we would lose this forest. Merton's words in a letter to his friend Jim Forest helped.

> Do not depend on the hope of results...You may have to face the fact that your work will be apparently worthless and even achieve no result at all, if not perhaps results opposite to what you expect. As you get used to this idea, you start more and more to concentrate not on the results, but on the value, the rightness, the truth of the work itself.[9]

Without attachment to outcomes, an activist acts in the paradox of unknowing. Yet there is always the consolation that nature holds us within a larger story, a more expansive narrative, and that somehow our words and actions matter. W.H. Auden's famous line in "In Memory of W.B. Yeats, "For poetry makes nothing happen," is often taken out of context, for Auden continues,

> ...it [poetry] survives
> In the valley of its making where executives

Would never want to tamper, flows on south
From ranches of isolation and the busy griefs,
Raw towns that we believe and die in; it survives,
A way of happening, a mouth.[10]

Poetry, this collective "mouth," this "way of happening," this "larger conversation," has the hidden capacity to change consciousness, and a change in consciousness can change the world, just as old Han Shan himself could have told us.[11]

Merton and the Trees

Besides the spirit of Han Shan, I brought along into our endangered forest the tree lover and early ecologist Thomas Merton, whose journals are punctuated with references to deer, birds, and trees. From the time of his earliest writing until his death, Merton expresses a sacramental vision of nature. In 1963 he corresponded with the environmental activist Rachel Carson, author of the bestselling indictment of the widespread use of pesticides, *Silent Spring* (1962).[12] Monica Weis, in her seminal study, *The Environmental Vision of Thomas Merton*, explores the childhood roots and lifelong development of Merton's ecological concerns.[13]

From the start Merton wasn't interested in trees and birds in the abstract, but in all their wondrous particularity.

This particular tree will give glory to God by spreading out
its roots in the earth and raising its branches into the air
and the light in a way that no other tree before or after it
ever did or will do.[14]

In his journal entries of June 1952, we find Merton working out what we now call an environmental ethic. His call to the contemplative life is simultaneously a call to ecological balance and restoration. During the 1950s he found himself involved in tree-planting activities at the monastery. When I was wandering through our local forest placing poems on trees, I recalled Merton's tree-planting days, his desire for reparation and healing, his need to connect with nature's inherent powers of renewal. Since Merton's time, many scientists and artists have confirmed, as Merton suggests, that trees are sentient life forms, consciousness, elders, lungs of the planet, companions.

In a July 1956 journal entry Merton observes,

> We do not realize that the fields and the trees have fought and still fight for their respective places on this map...We do not remember that these little clumps and groves are the fifth column of the aboriginal forest that wants to return. It is nice to think of, for a moment... I am perhaps still on the side of the trees.[15]

A few years later in May 1965 (before meeting Margie) he expounds his reasons for choosing a solitary life in the woods.

> It is necessary for me to live here alone...for the silence of the forest is my bride and the sweet dark warmth of the whole world is my love, and out of the heart of that dark warmth comes the secret that is heard only in silence, but it is the root of all the secrets that are whispered by all the lovers in their beds all over the world. I have an obligation to preserve the stillness, the silence, the poverty, the virginal point of pure nothingness which is at the centre of all other loves. I cultivate this plant silently in the middle of the night and water it with psalms and prophecies in silence. It becomes the most beautiful of all the trees in the garden, at once the primordial paradise tree, the *axis mundi*, the cosmic axle, and the Cross.[16]

Whether approaching nature as a solitary or through our shared human intimacies, Merton's sense of interconnection with the natural world was not merely a simple pantheism that argues God and nature are identical, but a vision that locates nature, humans, other species, and the divine within a dynamic, indissoluble, and interactive unity. I dwell in you and you in me and all us together within a more inclusive and loving reality. The term "panentheism," coined by German philosopher Karl Friedrich Krause (1791-1832), is perhaps closer to Merton's sense of how the temporal and eternal worlds are interrelated, held in a more inclusive mystery where inter-being plays at many levels. I would call Merton a unitive mystic.

Merton, influenced by William Blake and the Romantics, as well as medieval mystics, sages, and wisdom teachers East and West, felt contemplation of the "thusness" of nature could open us to participation in what he called God, ultimate Being itself, in both its personal and transpersonal dimensions. The theologian Duns Scotus speaks of *haecceity* (thusness) as nature participating in this larger whole precisely by virtue of being fully itself. Merton's love of nature ties to his paradisiacal vision of our primal unity with all things. For him, to cut ourselves off from nature, or to exploit it for our own limited ends, not only desecrated (de-sacralised) nature but undermined the matrix that sustains us. For Merton, Sophia or Holy Wisdom is incarnate in nature as *natura naturans*, or nature doing what nature does, which is being herself and acting as the essential creative power within us and the world.

Now it seems to me that Sophia, Merton, and the trees led me to a place beyond gender divisiveness, a place as inclusive as the Great Imagination itself; a place where variously gendered and trans-gendered energies interweave and a place from which they spring; a place from which green music emanates and the place it returns to, embraced by the all-encompassing silence that is Love.

1   Thomas Merton, *New Seeds of Contemplation* (Boston, Mass.: Shambhala, 1961), 33.

2   Thomas Merton, *Contemplation in a World of Action*, Foreword Robert Coles (Notre Dame, Indiana: University of Notre Dame Press, 1998), 139.

3   Citations from Merton's "Hagia Sophia" are drawn from *In the Dark Before Dawn: New Selected Poems of Thomas Merton*, ed. Lynn R. Szabo (NY: New Directions, 2005), 65-71.

4   An earlier version of this subsection first appeared in my memoir *Into the Mystic: My Years with Olga* (Toronto: Inanna Publications, 2014), 192-195.

5   Merton, "Hagia Sophia," *In the Dark Before Dawn*, 65.

6   Ibid.

7   An earlier and shorter version of this subsection appeared as "Art and Activism: How an ancient poet inspired a local initiative to preserve McLellan Forest," in *Common Ground* (March 2013), http://commonground.ca/2013/03/art-activism/

8   Merton, "Merlin and the Deer," *In the Dark Before Dawn*, 44.

9   Thomas Merton, letter dated Feb. 21, 1966 to James Forest in *The Hidden Ground of Love*, ed. William H. Shannon (New York: Farrar, Straus, Giroux, 1985), 294.

10   W.H. Auden, *Selected Poetry of W.H. Auden* (NY: Random House, 1958), 53.

11   Tim Lilburn, *The Larger Conversation: Contemplation and Place* (Edmonton, Alberta: Univ. of Edmonton Press, 2017). The phrase "the larger conversation" is drawn from Lilburn's reflections on human alienation from the earth and how lost or forgotten ancient esoteric and mystical traditions might help lead us home.

12   Thomas Merton, "To Rachel Carson," in *Thomas Merton: Witness to Freedom: Letters in Times of Crisis*, ed. William H. Shannon (San Diego: Harcourt Brace & Co., 1994), 70-72.

13   Monica Weis, SSJ, *The Environmental Vison of Thomas Merton* (Lexington, Kentucky: University Press of Kentucky, 2011). Weis cites Brother Patrick Hart, one of Merton's novices, who writes that Merton regarded the woods as "a sacrament of God's presence and was concerned about preserving it not only for our generation, but for generations to come" (137).

14   Thomas Merton, *New Seeds of Contemplation*, 31.

15   Thomas Merton, *A Search for Solitude: The Journals of Thomas Merton*, Vol. 3: 1952-1960, ed. Lawrence S. Cunningham (San Francisco: Harper Collins, 1966), 51.

16   Thomas Merton, *Dancing in the Water of Life: The Journals of Thomas Merton*, Vol.5: 1963-1965, ed. Robert E. Daggy (NY: HarperSanFrancisco, 1998), 240.

Afterword

Celebrating a Poet's Legacy
for His Artful Readers

> My vocation and task in this world is to keep alive all that is
> usefully individual and personal to me, to be a 'contempla-
> tive' in the full sense and to share it with others, to remain
> as a witness to the nobility of the private person and his [or
> her] primacy over the group.
> — Thomas Merton, *A Search for Solitude*

As I casually opened Merton's autobiography, taking it up from
my uncle's bedside table, I could not have realized the long journey of instruction in the art of living that I was so innocently
commencing at age 13. And now, as I matriculate into the studies of my seventh decade, Thomas Merton still privately tutors
me in who I might yet be, on the very cusp of my ceasing to be
who I am at all. I have appreciated the existence of my most
intimate selves while in the school of this monk's artful exhibi-
tions of his own inner experiences. As I have dialogued with
Merton's texts, and even with their silences, I have been shown
paths to becoming my own true self; and then, beyond these,
the further paths to losing my own self and becoming someone
wholly more.

Reading Merton has coached me in the practices of those he described in *New Seeds of Contemplation* as "contemplatives," who are first and foremost "fully alive and awake." His summons to wake up to the joys of being a human being has pressed me to keep hearing his voice. Through him I have learned to receive each day as an opportunity to live a deeper and more gracefully inclusive life. In the light of his counsel, I have also imbibed sad but necessary truths: I am deeply flawed and unfinished, a beginner always far from achieving high degrees. To steal by paraphrasing a line of Mary Oliver from her famous poem "The Summer Day," "I don't know what contemplation really is, but I shall not cease learning how to pay attention."

This collaboration by Susan McCaslin and J.S. Porter has encouraged my realizing again the value of Merton's legacy for his most dedicated and artful readers. This book has particularly revealed the creative sparks Merton ignites in his fellow poets who are striving to collaboratively express their lives of being "awake." In essays, poems, and conversations, McCaslin and Porter have exposed their vulnerabilities and debts to Merton's equally full and vulnerable disclosures. Singly and together, their voices here have sung in deep friendship with Merton's texts, but they have deployed their affections critically and have proven themselves poet-scholars of great maturity. While their book has shown full attention to their craft, the authors have yielded up an abundance of multi-hued insights into love and living that always attend a good show of personal, verbal fireworks.

What Merton wrote about John Henry Cardinal Newman describes the effects he elicits in many of his most dedicated readers. "There are people one meets in books or in life whom one does not merely observe, meet or know. A deep resonance of one's entire being is immediately set up with the entire being of the other (*Cor ad cor loquitur*) – heart speaks to heart in the wholeness of the language of music; true friendship is a kind of singing" (*Conjectures of a Guilty Bystander*).

As I close in celebrating the blending of these two poets' voices with Merton's own, I sing my best wishes for the journeys of instruction to be undertaken by Merton's future readers; his voice will slowly rise up to join with theirs and resonate. Merton wrote that he wanted to speak to his reader as his reader's "own self." While he admitted he didn't know what that might mean, he nevertheless intuited that what a reader found most deeply valuable in Merton's voice and life would be in communion with what was most deeply valuable in his reader's voice and life. A single voice singing out loud of its search for a superabundantly awake life is beautiful, but only achieves its perfection by joining a choir of other voices that revel most in being side-by-side as they search for all the songs they can sing in harmony.

Bibliography

Arasteh, A. Riza. *Final Integration in the Adult Personality*. Leiden, Netherlands: E.J. Brill, 1965.

Auden, W.H. *Selected Poetry of W.H. Auden*. New York: Random House, 1958.

Baciu, Stefan. "The Literary Catalyst," in *Continuum: In Memory of Thomas Merton*. Vol. 7, No. 2, Summer 1969.

Berger, John. *Keeping a Rendezvous*. New York: Pantheon Books, 1991.

Cardenal, Ernesto. *The Gospel in Art by the Peasants of Solentiname*. Eds. Philip and Sally Scharper. Maryknoll, New York: Orbis Books, 1984.

Cohen, Leonard. *Beautiful Losers*. Toronto: McClelland & Stewart, 1966.

———. *Book of Longing*. Toronto: McClelland & Stewart, 2006.

———. *Stranger Music: Selected Poems and Songs*. Toronto: McClelland & Stewart, 1993.

Douglass, James. W. *JFK and The Unspeakable: Why He Died & Why It Matters*. New York: Orbis Books, 2008.

Dylan, Bob. "It's Alright, Ma (I'm Only Bleeding)." <www. bobdylan.com/songs/its-alright-ma-im-only-bleeding>. Accessed March 30, 2016.

Elie, Paul. *The Life You Save May Be Your Own: An American Pilgrimage*. Maryknoll, NY: Orbis Books, 2003.

Emerson, Ralph Waldo. *Emerson in his Journals*. Selected and edited by Joel Porte. Cambridge, Mass.: Belknap Press/Harvard Univ. Press, 1982.

———. *Nature and Selected Essays*. Edited with an Introduction by Larzer Ziff. London: Penguin, 2003.

Evdokimov, Paul. *Woman and the Salvation of the World*. Crestwood, New York: St. Vladimir's Seminary Press, 1994.

Forest, Jim. *Living With Wisdom: A Life of Thomas Merton*. New York: Orbis Books, 1991.

———. *Praying with Icons*. Maryknoll, New York: Orbis Books, 1997.

Friedan, Betty. *The Feminine Mystique*. Introd. Gail Collins. NY: W.W. Norton, 2013.

Furlong, Monica. *Merton: A Biography*. London: Collins, 1980.

Georgiou, S.T. *The Way of the Dreamcatcher: Spirit Lessons with Robert Lax: Poet, Peacemaker, Sage*. Ottawa, Ontario: Novalis, 2002.

Griffin, John Howard. *Follow the Ecstasy: Thomas Merton, The Hermitage Years, 1965-1968*. Fort Worth, Texas: JHG Editions/Latitudes Press, 1983.

Hart, Brother Patrick. Online interview with Sister Mary Margaret Funk conducted on December 6, 2004. <http://www.dimmid.org/index.asp?Type=B_BASIC&SEC=%7B447E6A59-F5AC-4F91-A28F-183A90AC68E6%7D>. Accessed March 30, 2016.

Harford, James. *Merton & Friends: A Joint Biography of Thomas Merton, Robert Lax, and Edward Rice*. New York: Continuum, 2006.

Hemingway, Ernest. <www.profilesinhistory.com/flipbooks/Historical_84/files/.../ page84.html>. Accessed March 30, 2016.

Heaney, Seamus. *Station Island*. London: Faber and Faber, 1984.

Higgins, Michael W. *Heretic Blood: The Spiritual Geography of Thomas Merton*. Toronto: Stoddart, 1998.

——. *Stalking the Holy: The Pursuit of Saint Making*. Toronto: House of Anansi, 2006.

Hirsch, Edward. *The Living Fire: New and Selected Poems*. New York: Knopf, 2013.

Inchausti, Robert. *Thomas Merton's American Prophecy*. Albany, New York: SUNY, 1998.

Jung, Carl. <http://jungcurrents.com/importance-assumption-virgin-mary>. Accessed March 30, 2016.

Kazantzakis, Nikos. *Zorba the Greek*. Trans. Carl Wildman. London: Faber and Faber, 1961.

Kunitz, Stanley with Genine Lentine. *The Wild Braid: A Poet Reflects on a Century in the Garden*. New York: W.W. Norton & Co., 2005.

Kundera, Milan. *Encounter*. Translated by Linda Asher. New York: Harper, 2009.

Labrie, Ross. *The Art of Thomas Merton*. Fort Worth: Texas Christian University Press, 1979.

Lax, Robert. *Journal C*. Zurich: Pendo, 1990.

——. "Harpo's Progress: Towards an Understanding of Merton's Ways," in *The Merton Annual: Studies in Thomas Merton, Religion, Culture, Literature & Social Concerns*. Vol. 1. New York: AMS Press, 1988.

——. "Remembering Thomas Merton & New York," in *The Merton Annual: Studies in Thomas Merton, Religion, Culture, Literature & Social Concerns*. Vol. 5. New York: AMS Press, 1992.

Lentfoehr, Sister Therese. *Words and Silence: On the Poetry of Thomas Merton*. New York: New Directions, 1979.

Levertov, Denise. *Breathing the Water*. New York: New Directions, 1992.

——. *Denise Levertov: Poems 1960-1967*. New York: New Directions, 1966.

——. *Denise Levertov: Poems 1968-1972*. New York: New Directions, 1978.

——. *Evening Train*. New York: New Directions, 1992.

——. *The Letters of Robert Duncan and Denise Levertov*. Eds. Robert J. Bertholf and Albert Gelpi. Stanford, CA: Stanford University Press, 2004.

——. *Making Peace*. Ed. Peggy Rosenthal. New York: New Directions, 2006.

——. *New and Selected Essays*. New York: New Directions, 1992.

——. *Oblique Prayers*. New York: New Directions, 1984.

——. *The Poet in the World*. New York: New Directions, 1973.

——. *Relearning the Alphabet*. New York: New Directions, 1966.

——. *Sands of the Well*. New York: New Directions, 1996.

Lilburn, Tim. *The Larger Conversation: Contemplation and Place*. Edmonton, Alberta: University of Alberta Press, 2017.

Lipsey, Roger. *Angelic Mistakes: The Art of Thomas Merton*. Foreword Paul M. Pearson. Boston: New Seeds/Shambhala Publications, 2006.

MacNiven, Ian S. *"Literchoor is My Beat": A Life of James Laughlin, Publisher of New Directions*. New York: Farrar, Straus and Giroux, 2014.

Malits, Elena C.S.o.C. *The Solitary Explorer: Thomas Merton's Transforming Journey*. San Francisco: Harper and Row, 1980.

Marley, Ziggy. "Justice." http://www.melodymakers.com/music/songs/ songs.cgi?justice.

Matthews, Caitlin. *Sophia, Goddess of Wisdom: The Divine Feminine from Black Goddess to World-Soul*. Hammersmith, London: Mandala Press, 1991.

McCaslin, Susan. "Art and Activism: How an Ancient Poet Inspired a Local Initiative to Preserve McLellan Forest." *Common Ground* (March 2013). <http:// commonground.ca/2013/03/art-activism/>.

——. "A Dream of Thomas Merton," in *Presence: An International Journal of Spiritual Direction*. Vol. 12, No. 3 (Sept. 2006), Vol. 21, No. 2 (June 2015), and Susan McCaslin's *Lifting the Stone*. Hamilton, Ontario: Seraphim Editions, 2007.

——. *Into the Mystic: My Years with Olga*. Toronto: Inanna Publications, 2014.

——. *A Matter of Spirit: Recovery of the Sacred in Contemporary Canadian Poetry*. Victoria, B.C.: Ekstasis Editions, 1998.

——. "Merton and Hagia Sophia (Holy Wisdom)," in *Merton & Hesychasm: The Prayer of the Heart*. Eds. Bernadette Dieker and Jonathan Montaldo. Louisville, Kentucky: Fons Vitae, 2003, 235-260.

——. "The Problem with Perfect," in *Arousing the Spirit: Provocative Writings*. Kelowna, BC, Canada: Wood Lake Publishing, 2011.

——. "Thomas Merton, Citizen of the World, Or Why Merton Matters Now," in *We Are Already One: Thomas Merton's Message of Hope: Reflections to Honor His Centenary*. Eds. Gray Henry and Jonathan Montaldo. Foreword Paul M. Pearson. Louisville, Kentucky: Fons Vitae, 2014.

McGregor, Michael N. *Pure Act: The Uncommon Life of Robert Lax*. New York: Fordham University Press, 2015.

Meatyard, Ralph Eugene. *Father Louie: Photographs of Thomas Merton*. With an Essay by Guy Davenport. Ed. Barry Magid. New York: Tinken Publishers, 1991.

Merleau-Ponty, Maurice. *The World of Perception*. Trans. Oliver Davis. London: Routledge, 2004.

Merton, Thomas. *The Asian Journal of Thomas Merton*. Eds. Naomi Burton, Brother Patrick Hart, & James Laughlin. NY: New Directions, 1968, 1975.

——. *Cold War Letters*. Eds. Christine M. Bochen and William H. Shannon. Foreword James W. Douglass. New York: Orbis Books, 2006.

——. *The Collected Poems of Thomas Merton*. New York: New Directions, 1977.

——. *Conjectures of a Guilty Bystander*. NY: Doubleday, 1968.

——. *Contemplation in a World of Action*. Foreword Robert Coles. Notre Dame, Indiana: University of Notre Dame Press, 1998.

——. *Contemplative Prayer*. Garden City, New York: Image/Doubleday, 1971.

——. *The Courage for Truth: Letters to Writers*. Ed. Christine M. Bochen. New York: Farrar, Straus and Giroux, 1993.

_____. *Dancing in the Water of Life: The Journals of Thomas Merton: Seeking Peace in the Hermitage*. Ed. Robert E. Daggy: 1963-1965. Vol. 5. NY: HarperSanFrancisco, 1998.

_____. "Day of a Stranger," in *Thomas Merton, Spiritual Master: The Essential Writings*. Ed. Lawrence Cunningham. NY: Paulist Press, 1992.

_____. *Day of a Stranger*. Introduction by Robert E. Daggy. Salt Lake City: Gibbs M. Smith, 1981.

_____. *Disputed Questions*. San Diego: Harcourt, Brace & Company, 1960.

_____. *Emblems of a Season of Fury*. New York: New Directions, 1963.

_____. *The Hidden Ground of Love: The Letters of Thomas Merton on Religious Experience and Social Concerns*. Ed. William H. Shannon; New York: Farrar, Straus, Giroux, 1985.

_____. *In the Dark Before Dawn: New Selected Poems of Thomas Merton*. Ed. Lynn R. Szabo. Preface Kathleen Norris. NY: New Directions, 2005.

_____. *Introductions East & West: The Foreign Prefaces of Thomas Merton*. Foreword Harry James Cargas. Oakville, Ontario: Mosaic Press, 1981.

_____. *Learning to Love: Exploring Solitude and Freedom: The Journals of Thomas Merton*: 1966-1967. Vol. 6. Ed. Christine M. Bochen. NY: HarperSanFrancisco, 1997.

_____. *The Literary Essays of Thomas Merton*. Ed. Brother Patrick Hart. New York: New Directions, 1960; 1981.

_____. *Love and Living*. Eds. Naomi Burton Stone and Brother Patrick Hart. San Diego: Harcourt Brace and Company, 1979.

_____. *Mystics and Zen Masters*. NY: The Noonday Press, 1967.

_____. *New Seeds of Contemplation*. Boston, Mass.: Shambhala, 1961; 2007.

_____. *New Seeds of Contemplation*. New York: New Directions, 1961.

_____. *No Man Is an Island*. New York: Image/Doubleday, 1967.

_____. *Opening the Bible*. Introduction by Rob Stone. Collegeville, Minn.: The Liturgical Press, 1986.

_____. *The Other Side of the Mountain: The End of the Journey: The Journals of Thomas Merton*. Vol. 7: 1967-1968. Ed. Patrick Hart. NY: HarperSanFrancisco, 1999.

_____. *Passion for Peace: The Social Essays*. Edited with an Introduction by William H. Shannon. New York: The Crossroad Publishing Company, 1997.

_____. *Raids on the Unspeakable*. New York: New Directions, 1964.

_____. *Run to the Mountain: The Story of a Vocation: The Journals of Thomas Merton*. Vol. 1: 1939-1941. Ed. Patrick Hart, O.C.S.O. NY: HarperSanFrancisco, 1995.

_____. *A Search for Solitude: The Journals of Thomas Merton: Pursuing the Monk's True Life*. Vol. 3: 1952-1960. Ed. Lawrence Cunningham. NY: HarperSanFrancisco, 1996.

_____. *The Secular Journal*. New York: Farrar, Straus & Giroux, 1959; 1977.

_____. *The Seven Storey Mountain*. NY: Harcourt, Brace & Co., 1948.

_____. *The Sign of Jonas*. San Diego: Harcourt Brace & Co., 1981.

_____. *Thomas Merton: The Hidden Ground of Love: The Letters of Thomas Merton on Religious Experience and Social Concerns.* Ed. William H. Shannon. NY: Farrar, Straus & Giroux, 1985.

_____. *Thomas Merton, Springs of Contemplation: A Retreat at the Abbey of Gethsemani.* Foreword Kathleen Norris. Notre Dame, Indiana: Ave Maria Press, 1992.

_____. *Thoughts in Solitude.* NY: Farrar, Straus & Giroux, 1999.

_____. "To Rachel Carson," in *Thomas Merton: Witness to Freedom: Letters in Times of Crisis.* Ed. William H. Shannon. San Diego: Harcourt Brace & Co., 1994.

_____. *Turning Toward the World: The Journals of Thomas Merton.* Vol. 4: 1960-1963. Ed. Victor A. Kramer. NY: HarperSanFrancisco, 1996.

_____. *Witness to Freedom: Letters in Times of Crisis.* Ed. William H. Shannon. San Diego: Harcourt Brace & Co., 1994.

_____. *Zen and the Birds of Appetite.* New York: New Directions, 1968.

Merton, Thomas and Robert Lax. *A Catch of Anti-Letters.* Foreword Brother Patrick Hart. Sheed & Ward, 1978; 1994.

Merton, Thomas and Rosemary Radford Ruether. *At Home in the World: The Letters of Thomas Merton & Rosemary Radford Ruether.* Ed. Mary Tardiff, OP. Introd. Rosemary Radford Ruether. Afterword Christine Bochen. New York: Orbis Books, 1995.

McKay, Don. *The Shell of the Tortoise: Four Essays & an Assemblage.* Kentville, NS: Gaspereau Press, 2011.

Montaldo, Jonathan, ed. *Dialogues with Silence: Prayers & Drawings.* NY: HarperCollins, 2001.

_____. "A Gallery of Women's Faces," in *The Merton Annual: Studies in Culture, Spirituality & Social Concerns.* Vol. 14. Sheffield Academic Press, 2001.

Moses, John. *Divine Discontent: The Prophetic Voice of Thomas Merton.* Foreword by Rowan Williams. London: Bloomsbury Publishing, 2014.

Mott, Michael. *The Seven Mountains of Thomas Merton.* Boston: Houghton Mifflin, 1984.

Oliver, Mary. *Dream Work.* New York: Atlantic Monthly Press, 1986.

——. *New and Selected Poems.* Boston: Beacon Press, 1992.

Piercy, Marge. *Available Light: Poems by Marge Piercy.* NY: Knopf, 1988.

Pope Francis, cited by Grant Gallicho. "Pope Francis to Congress: Be Your Best." *Commonweal.* 24 Sept. 2015. https://www.commonwealmagazine.org/blog/pope-francis-congress-be-your-best.

Pope Francis. Address to Congress. www.vox.com/2015/9/24/9391549/pope-remarks-full-text.

Poks, Malgorzata. "Encounter in a Secret Country: Thomas Merton and Jorge Carrera Andrade," in *The Merton Annual: Studies in Culture, Spirituality, and Social Concerns.* Vol. 18. Ed. Victor A. Kramer. Louisville: Fons Vitae, 2005.

Porter, J.S. *The Thomas Merton Poems: A Caravan of Poems.* Goderich, Ontario: Moonstone, 1988.

——. *Thomas Merton: Hermit at the Heart of Things*. Toronto: Novalis, 2008.

Pramuk, Christopher. *At Play in Creation: Merton's Awakening to the Feminine*. Order of St. Benedict, Collegeville, Minnesota: Liturgical Press, 2015.

——. *Sophia: The Hidden Christ of Thomas Merton*. Collegeville, Minnesota: Liturgical Press, 2009.

Rice, Edward. *The Man in the Sycamore Tree: The Good Times and Hard Life of Thomas Merton: An Entertainment with Photographs*. New York: Image/Doubleday, 1972.

——. "Portrait of Thomas Merton." <http://www.therealmerton.com/>. Accessed April 11, 2016.

Rilke, Rainer Maria. *Letters to a Young Poet*. Trans. Stephen Mitchell. NY: Random House, 1986.

——. *Selected Poems*. Trans. with an Introduction J.B. Leishman. London: Penguin, 1964.

——. *Rilke: Selected Poems*. Trans. C.F. MacIntyre. Oakland, California: University of California Press, 1957.

Rilke, Rainer Maria and Maurice Betz. *Rilke in Paris*. Trans. Will Stone. London: Hesperus Press, 2012.

Ruether, Rosemary Radford. *Goddesses and the Divine Feminine: A Western Religious History*. Berkeley: University of California Press, 2005.

——. *Integrating Ecofeminism, Globalization and World Religions*. Toronto: Rowman & Littlefield, 2005.

——. *New Woman, New Earth: Sexist Ideologies and Human Liberation*. San Francisco: Harper & Row, 1975.

Seeger, Pete. "Turn Turn Turn." <http://www.lyricsmode.com/lyrics/p/pete_seeger/>. Accessed March 30, 2016.

Shannon, William H. *Silent Lamp: The Thomas Merton Story*. New York: Crossroad, 1992.

Shaw, Mark. *Beneath the Mask of Holiness*. NY: Palgrave Macmillan, 2009.

Smith, Huston. *And Live Rejoicing: Chapters from a Charmed Life*. Novato, California: New World Library, 2012.

Solovyov, Vladimir. *The Meaning of Love*. Introd. Owen Barfield. Hudson, New York: Lindisfarne Press, 1985.

Steindl-Rast Br., David. "Recollections of Thomas Merton's Last Days in the West," Notes made at a Meeting of Our Lady of the Redwoods, Whitehorn, CA. *Monastic Studies* 7.10 (1969) 1-10.

Stern, Karl. *The Flight from Woman*. NY: Farrar, Straus and Giroux, 1965.

Tardiff, Mary, OP, ed. *At Home in the World: the Letters of Thomas Merton & Rosemary Radford Ruether*. Maryknoll, New York: Orbis Books, 1995.

Tranströmer, Tomas. *The Half-Finished Heaven: The Best Poems of Tomas Tranströmer*. Selected & translated by Robert Bly. Minneapolis: Graywolf, 2001.

Waldron, Robert G. *The Exquisite Risk of Love: The Chronicle of a Monastic Romance*. London: Darton, Longman and Todd, 2012.

———. *Thomas Merton in Search of His Soul: A Jungian Perspective.* Notre Dame, Indiana: Ave Maria Press, 1994.

Weis, Monica, SSJ. *The Environmental Vision of Thomas Merton.* Lexington, Kentucky: University Press of Kentucky, 2011.

Whitman, Walt. *Leaves of Grass.* Introduction by Gay Wilson Allen. New York: New American Library, 1955; 1980.

Wilkes, Paul. *Merton By Those Who Knew Him Best.* San Francisco: Harper & Row, 1984.

Williams, C.K. *On Whitman.* Princeton: Princeton University Press, 2010.

Williams, Rowan. *A Silent Action: Engagements with Thomas Merton.* Louisville, Kentucky: Fons Vitae, 2010.

Woolf, Virginia. "Hours in the Library." <www.therumpus.net/2012/perceptive-and-prophetic>. Accessed March 31, 2016.

Yeats, W.B. "A Dialogue of Self and Soul," in *Collected Poems.* London: MacMillan & Co., 1969.

Acknowledgments

Susan McCaslin and J.S. Porter wish to thank Mike Schwartzentruber at Wood Lake Publishing, as well as members of the Wood Lake staff, for believing in this project from the outset and guiding us through the intricacies of the editorial and publishing process. We would especially like to thank Ellen Turnbull for walking us so expertly through the editing process.

SUSAN'S THANKS

Profound gratitude to:

- Writer, poet, and long-time friend J.S. Porter for entering with me into this superabundantly alive, engrossing, and energizing collaboration.
- Lynn R. Szabo for her astute and insightful Foreword and meticulous editing
- Jonathan Montaldo for his eloquent Afterword
- Afton Schindel for her innovative graphic designs for my suite of poems "A Grotto of Sophia Ikons"
- Mike Schwartzentruber and the Wood Lake team for believing in and supporting our collaboration from the start
- Ellen Turnbull, editor for Wood Lake, for her helpful input and meticulous editing of the manuscript
- Robert MacDonald for his elegant design and formatting of the manuscript
- Pattie Bender for her excellent proofreading skills
- Dr. Christopher Pramuk for his inspiring critical work on the sophianic depths of Merton's body of work
- Members of The Thomas Merton Society of Canada (the late Donald Grayston, Judith Hardcastle, Ross LaBrie, Ron Dart, Angus Stuart, et al.) for their support
- Antoinette Voûte Roeder, author of *Still Breathing; Poems for Meditation* and *The Many Singings* (Apocryphile Press) for feedback on early sections of the manuscript
- Dr. Michael W. Higgins for his support, encouragement, and his own inspiring work on Thomas Merton

I wish to acknowledge my indebtedness to Dr. Paul M. Pearson, Director and Archivist of the Thomas Merton Centre at Bellarmine University, for his vital assistance during the research process.

Most of all, I wish to thank my husband, Mark Haddock, for his indispensable feedback and his willingness to live graciously with the lively ghost of Thomas Merton, and my daughter, Claire Haddock, for her commitment to the education of children.

JOHN'S THANKS

I'm very grateful to my friend Susan McCaslin for waking me from slumber and inviting me to join her in a word-dance on Thomas Merton. Her generosity and kindness are boundless.

Thanks to my wife Cheryl who has taught me the truth of Rabbi Heschel's words, "Just to be is a blessing. Just to live is holy."

Thanks to my mother whose encouragement to keep writing has been a constant in my life.

Thanks to Professor Lynn R. Szabo for treating the manuscript as if it were her own. Her attention to detail and dedication to exactitude are much appreciated. And thanks to Mark Haddock for his expertise, patience, and wisdom in preparing the manuscript for publication.

Thanks to Richard Whittaker at *Works & Conversations* (www.conversations.org) for his warm-hearted embrace of our dialogue on the feminine.

Thanks to Mike Schwartzentruber for believing that our book might belong with Wood Lake, and Ellen Turnbull for her kind, generous, and superb editing.

I'm also grateful to those who have given me a reason to write – Patrick O'Connell, editor of *The Merton Seasonal*; Nancy Duffy (www.thenancyduffyshow.com); Janet Hicks King (www.dialogue2.ca); and Paul Lisson & Fiona Kinsella, editors of *Hamilton Arts and Letters* magazine (www.samizdatpress.typepad.com) where I used the title "Thomas Merton, Superabundantly Alive" for an essay on Merton in *HA&L* Issue 2, 2009.

PERMISSIONS

"Hagia Sophia" by Thomas Merton, from *The Collected Poems of Thomas Merton*, copyright ©1963 by The Abbey of Gethsemani. Reprinted by permission of New Directions Publishing Corp.

Victor Hammer's line-cut image of Hagia Sophia. Reprinted by permission of Paul Holbrook, executor of the Hammer estate.

Previous Publication

The following pieces appeared previously in the following publications:

"Thomas Merton in Las Vegas" by J.S. Porter in *The Merton Seasonal*, Summer 1991 (Vol. 16, No. 3), 9.

"Merton and Hagia Sophia (Holy Wisdom)," in *Merton & Hesychasm: the Prayer of the Heart*. Eds. Bernadette Dieker and Jonathan Montaldo. Louisville, Kentucky: Fons Vitae, 2003, 235-260.

"A Dream of Thomas Merton" by Susan McCaslin in *Presence: An International Journal of Spiritual Direction*. Vol. 12, No. 3 (Sept. 2006), 20. Grand Prize winner of their annual poetry contest. It appeared subsequently in *The Merton Journal: Journal of the Thomas Merton Society of Great Britain & Ireland* (Vol. 14, No. 2; 2007), and was again reprinted in *Presence* (Vol. 21, No. 2, June 2015). The poem is also included in McCaslin's volume of poetry *Lifting the Stone*. Hamilton, Ontario: Seraphim Editions, 2007.

"Pivoting Toward Peace: the Engaged Poetics of Thomas Merton and Denise Levertov" by Susan McCaslin in: *The Pacific Rim Review of Books*. Victoria, B.C. Issue 10 (Fall/Winter 2009); *The Merton Annual*. Louisville, Kentucky. *Fons Vitae* (Vol. 22, 2009); *Along the Rim: the Best of the Pacific Rim Review of Books*. Vol. 2. Eds. Trevor Carolan and Richard Olafson. Introd. Paul E. Nelson. Victoria, B.C.: Ekstasis Editions, 2010.

"Why Merton Matters Now" by Susan McCaslin as "Thomas Merton, Citizen of the World, Or Why Merton Matters Now" in *We Are Already One: Thomas Merton's Message of Hope, Reflections to Honor His Centenary*. Eds. Gray Henry and Jonathan Montaldo. Foreword Paul M. Pearson. Louisville, Kentucky: Fons Vitae, 2014.

"The Divine and Embodied Feminine: A Dialogue" by Susan McCaslin & J.S. Porter in *Works & Conversations*. Ed. Richard Whittaker. Jan. 18, 2018. http://www.conversations.org/story.php?sid=547

Author Biographies

Susan McCaslin (Ph.D., University of British Columbia) is a poet and Thomas Merton scholar who has published 15 volumes of poetry, including poetic sequences on Thomas Merton. She taught English and Creative Writing at Douglas College in New Westminster, British Columbia for 23 years. Susan has published a variety of critical studies on Merton, including those in *Merton and Hesychasm* (Fons Vitae), and *We Are Already One: Thomas Merton's Message of Hope; Reflections to Honour His Centenary* (1915-2015). She has authored a volume of essays, *Arousing the Spirit: Provocative Writings* (Wood Lake, 2011), and a memoir, *Into the Mystic: My Years with Olga* (Inanna, 2014). Her most recent volumes of poetry are *Into the Open: Poems New and Selected* (Inanna, 2017) and *Painter, Poet, Mountain: After Cézanne* (Quattro Books, 2016). Susan resides in Fort Langley, BC with her husband, Mark. www.susanmccaslin.ca

J.S. Porter was born in Belfast in the north of Ireland and educated at McMaster University (MA in English Literature) in Hamilton, Ontario. He has written about Thomas Merton in *The Merton Seasonal*, *The Merton Annual*, and *The Merton Journal*, as well as in *Brick*, *Grail*, *The Nashwaak Review*, and *The Antigonish Review*. Culture critic for The Nancy Duffy Show, he is a columnist for *Dialogue Magazine* and a frequent contributor to the online journal *Hamilton Arts and Letters*. His books about Merton include: *The Thomas Merton Poems* (Moonstone, 2008) and *Thomas Merton: Hermit at the Heart of Things* (Novalis, 2008). He is also the author of *Spirit Book Word: An Inquiry into Literature and Spirituality*, *The Glass Art of Sarah Hall*, and *Of Wine and Reading*, a poetry chapbook published by the Alfred Gustav Press in Vancouver in 2016. He lives in Hamilton, Ontario with his wife, Cheryl. www.spiritbookword.net

ALSO AVAILABLE FROM WOOD LAKE

Passion & Peace

The Poetry of Uplift for All Occasions

Compiled by Diane Tucker

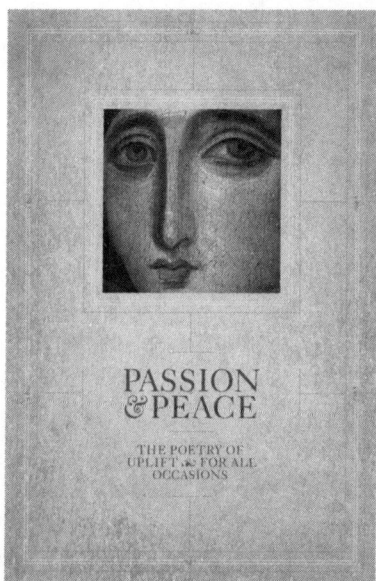

All cultures we know of, at all times, have had poetry of one sort or another – chants, songs, lullabies, epics, blessings, farewells – to mark life's most important moments, transitions, and transformations. Ever since our species began using words, we have arranged them to please, to experience the pleasures, the fun, of rhythm and rhymn, repetition and pattern. *Passion & Peace: The Poetry of Uplift for All Occasions* was compiled to speak directly to this deep human need, with 120 of best poems from almost as many classical and contemporary poets, and including a thematic index. A welcome addition to any library and the perfect gift for any occasion, *Passion & Peace* is a heartwarming, uplifting, and inspirational volume.

ISBN 978-1-77343-028-7

6" x 9" | 304 PP | $24.95

WOOD LAKE

**IMAGINING, LIVING, AND TELLING
THE FAITH STORY.**

Wood Lake is the faith story company.

It has told
- the story of the seasons of the earth, the people of God, and the place and purpose of faith in the world;
- the story of the faith journey, from birth to death;
- the story of Jesus and the churches that carry his message.

Wood Lake has been telling stories for more than 35 years. During that time, it has given form and substance to the words, songs, pictures, and ideas of hundreds of storytellers.

Those stories have taken a multitude of forms – parables, poems, drawings, prayers, epiphanies, songs, books, paintings, hymns, curricula – all driven by a common mission of serving those on the faith journey.

WOOD LAKE PUBLISHING INC.
485 Beaver Lake Road
Kelowna, BC, Canada v4v 1s5
250.766.2778

www.woodlake.com